Personnel Management in Associations

A Guide to Staff and
Volunteer Organization,
Job Description, and
Salary Administration

Gerald L. McManis
Jerrie A. Stewart
McManis Associates, Inc.

American Society of Association Executives

Copyright © 1980 by the American Society of Association Executives, 1575 Eye Street, NW, Washington, D.C. 20005-1168. All Rights Reserved.
Second Printing, 1988.
International Standard Book Number: 0-88034-010-X
Manufactured in the United States of America.

Preface

The essential skill that lies at the heart of the job of an association executive is the ability to motivate, organize, and manage people. Human resources are the greatest asset any association has, and the effective mobilization of those resources is central to the success or failure of an association.

This book is designed to help association executives develop their people-moving skills. It includes techniques and opinions on motivating, developing, and rewarding both staff and volunteers.

ASAE is grateful to McManis Associates for its superb effort in making this excellent contribution to the literature of the field of association management.

Table of Contents

Preface

Contents

Introduction

Chapter I
The Role of Volunteer Leaders in Associations 11
Model Position Descriptions for Association Volunteers 21

Chapter II
The Role of the Professional Staff 25

Chapter III
Organization for Management 33

Chapter IV
Defining Responsibilities: The Position Description 55
Model Position Descriptions for Association Staff 67

Chapter V
Staff Compensation 105

Chapter VI
Personnel Management 121

Bibliography 139

Introduction

The 1980s will be a decade of challenge. Many predictions for the future suggest that a variety of social and economic conditions will challenge the "American way of life" as we know it today. Noted economists tell us that we can expect continued inflation, soaring energy costs, and further reduction of disposable income. This less-than-optimistic economic forecast has critical implications for associations. It means that association members will more often ask: "What are we getting for our dues?" All types of members will question the value and the effectiveness of associations—the companies and corporations that support trade associations as well as the teachers, doctors, and scientists who join professional societies.

Not only will they raise questions about the current level of service, but they will expect the association to provide more services to help them cope with social and economic changes. And, because of the financial constraints they face, they will resist paying more for additional services. Their resistance will be reinforced by the general skepticism toward public and nonprofit institutions that ushered out the 1970s and was reflected in Proposition 13 and other taxpayer-supported movements to reduce public spending.

These challenges will affect both the professional association executives and the volunteer leaders of associations. The volunteer leaders will feel the pressure from members who seek more services without corresponding dues increases and who demand greater effectiveness and efficiency in the performance of the association. Some members may even expect that the volunteer leadership should not only have intimate knowledge of how membership dollars are spent but that they should "get involved" to ensure effectiveness in internal operations.

This expectation has potentially dangerous implications for professional association management. Therefore, it is critical that volunteer leaders understand their governance role. They must recognize the means to fulfill their fiduciary responsibilities and enhance the effectiveness of their association without becoming involved in internal operations. Conversely, the chief staff executive and the paid staff of the association must be able to demonstrate to the volunteer leaders and the members at large that they are maximizing the use of the association's resources. Clearly, the most valuable of these resources are the people involved in the association—both the volunteers and the staff.

To be effective in the 1980s, association executives must be more innovative and resourceful in developing and using the human resources of their organizations. They must be able to determine how best to encourage and enhance the performance of the volunteers and maintain their strong support for the association. Internally, they must provide the leadership and direction necessary to realize and maximize the full potential of the staff. This responsibility presents many management challenges. The chief staff executive must determine how to:

- Organize staff functions;
- Ensure that all employees know what is expected of them;
- Establish an equitable compensation system in a nonprofit environment that will motivate and reward staff; and
- Train and develop employees in order to maintain a growing, dynamic staff organization.

This book on personnel management is designed to aid association executives and volunteer leaders in making the best use of the association's human resources. For the volunteer, the book provides guidance on the role of the association board of directors and the individual leaders. The first chapter identifies typical weaknesses in leadership activities and presents guidelines for effective performance. It also explores the relationship between the board and the association staff in order to help both groups understand and fulfill their appropriate roles.

For the association executive, *Personnel Management in Associations* provides a ready source of reference on many of the basic issues inherent in effective association management. The book discusses the role and responsibilities of different types and levels of staff. It explores the difficult task of organizing the staff at different stages in an association's evolutionary development and presents models for organizational structures. A full chapter is devoted to the important process of defining and documenting staff responsibilities through the development of position descriptions. It includes an extensive set of sample job descriptions for most of the positions commonly found in associations. Another chapter addresses one of the most frequently discussed topics in associations—staff compensation. It includes descriptions of various methods of position evaluation and salary administration. Finally, the last chapter describes additional elements of effective personnel management: staff screening and selection, personnel recordkeeping, training and development, and performance appraisal.

In addition to the management guidance in the book, a general bibliography on personnel management topics is provided, along with a list of other ASAE books, articles, and cassettes that address personnel management issues.

> *Personnel Management in Associations* was developed for ASAE by Gerald L. McManis and Jerrie A. Stewart of McManis Associates, Inc., management and research consultants. McManis Associates is headquartered in Washington, D.C. and maintains an office in San Francisco. The firm, which has a staff of 55, serves a diverse group of client organizations: professional, educational, and trade associations, foundations, colleges and universities, government agencies, and business and industrial firms.
>
> Mr. McManis, who is president of the firm, has provided management counsel to a large number of associations since the company was founded in 1964. Ms. Stewart, director of the Association Division of McManis, has worked with numerous trade and professional associations since joining the firm in 1974. The Association Division provides a wide range of services including organizational and management analysis, membership needs assessment, strategic planning, board and staff orientation, relocation planning, management information and word processing systems, and executive recruiting.

Chapter I

THE ROLE OF VOLUNTEER LEADERS IN ASSOCIATIONS

This chapter discusses the role of volunteer leaders in associations in the context of the challenges they will face in the 1980s and presents sample position descriptions for officers and other leaders. It also explores common weaknesses in board performance given the requirements for effective leadership and offers guidelines for strengthening it.

Volunteer Leadership in the 1980s

Volunteer leaders will face major challenges in the 1980s. Trade associations and professional societies will continue to grow and to play an increasingly important role in modern society. They will help their constituents respond to rapidly changing social and economic conditions and ever-expanding government regulation. They will serve as important vehicles for the effective exchange of new ideas and information in a world increasingly dependent upon changing technology. Associations will also continue to afford their members opportunities for peer recognition through election to leadership positions, but those volunteer leaders will be expected to play a more vital role in affecting the future and safeguarding the interests of their industries, institutions, or professions.

Volunteer leaders are in positions to influence the expenditure of billions of dollars towards research, education, and representational activities. They can set a tone and direction that will have a far-reaching impact on the profession or industry of which they are a part, as well as on society as a whole. Their actions can affect new technology, the training and development of the professions, and the passage of federal and state legislation and regulations.

Unfortunately, in the past, many volunteer leaders have viewed their elected offices as honorary positions, content that their responsibilities were fulfilled through regular attendance at meetings and social events sponsored by the association. But as associations are called upon to play an increasingly important role in society, they will demand a new breed of volunteer leaders. It will be critical to clearly define the role and responsibilities of those leaders in order to select the most qualified people to fill the positions. Traditionally, most associations have not done a good job in defining, documenting, and communicating the role volunteer leaders are expected to play. As a result, even after years of membership and service on committees, many elected leaders may come into office with little understanding of the role and responsibilities they are expected to fulfill.

Role of the Board

Ultimate responsibility for the association rests with the board of directors. The responsibility is recognized by state and federal laws; legally, the board is responsible for the activities, employees and fiscal integrity of the association. The appropriate role of the board is to set policies which will ensure that it fulfills its legal and professional responsibilities to the association. The board should set the tone for dynamic and aggressive leadership within the association.

The specific responsibility areas of the board are:

- Ensuring that the needs of the membership are met;
- Approving and evaluating programs and activities of the association;
- Planning the future direction of the association;
- Establishing broad policies to guide the operation of the association;
- Selecting and hiring the chief staff executive and monitoring and evaluating the staff executive's performance; and
- Setting financial objectives and monitoring their achievement.

These responsibilities are performed by the board as a whole. Clearly, the board cannot accomplish them without support and cooperation from the chief staff executive. Therefore, the relationship between the board, the chairman in particular, and the chief staff officer is critical to the effective performance of the board and to the success of the association. This relationship must be based on mutual respect and trust, and the lines between the authority of the board and of the chief staff executive must be clearly defined and adhered to.

Roles of Officers

In addition to sharing in the performance of the board as a whole, individual officers and volunteer leaders have specific roles to play in the governance and direction of the association. The responsibilities of the leadership positions and the titles they carry vary greatly from association to association. Generally, they are determined by a variety of factors: the size of the association, the nature of the membership, unique operating characteristics, decisions to broaden participation in the leadership, efforts to distribute the volunteer workload, and the latest trends among associations.

Despite the wide variety in assigned duties among volunteer leaders, there are a number of basic governance functions which are performed in all associations. And there are essentially two basic title structures for *volunteer* association officers. If the chief paid executive position carries the title "executive secretary," "executive director," or "executive vice president," the chief elected officer is usually called "president" and functions as chairman of the board. Then the other top officers in that title structure are likely to be "president elect," or "senior vice president" and "vice president" or "first vice president" and "second vice president." If the paid executive is the president, then the chief elected officer usually carries the title "chairman of the board." In that case, the other top elected officers are "senior vice chairman" or "chairman-elect" and "vice chairman" or "first vice chairman" and "second vice chairman." The other traditional leadership positions, such as "secretary" and "treasurer" usually carry the same title in most associations regardless of the title for the top officers.

The roles of the traditional officers in associations are, briefly:

- **President or Chairman.** Serves as chief elected officer of the association, directs other officers, presides as Chairman over all board actions, chairs the executive committee and may act as chief spokesman for the association.
- **Senior or First Vice President** (or President-Elect or Senior Vice Chairman). Assumes the responsibilities of the Chairman in his or her absence and performs special functions as assigned to assist the Chairman in performing the functions of that office; serves on the board and the executive committee. Most associations use this position to orient and groom the upcoming chief elected officer for his or her future role and responsibilities, particularly where the succession is automatic.
- **Vice President** (or Second Vice President or Second Vice Chairman). Serves as backup for the Senior Vice President; serves on the board and the executive committee; as requested, may support the President in performing his or her duties; and may chair one or more association committees.
- **Secretary.** Serves on the board and executive committee; ensures that records of all association, board, and executive committee meetings are maintained; may chair one or more association committees; and performs special functions as assigned.
- **Treasurer.** Oversees the fiscal affairs of the association and ensures that all financial records and audits are in order; serves on the board

and executive committee; usually serves on the finance committee; and performs special functions as assigned.

Model position descriptions for each of these officers are provided at the end of this chapter.

Role of the Individual Director

As noted at the outset of this chapter, the role of the board and thus of the individual board member will become increasingly challenging. It will not be enough for the director to fill his or her seat at board meetings and perform a perfunctory role in the association. The director must help to provide strong leadership for the association and to set a sound and accurate course for its future. It is important that the director realize that his or her role is to participate in setting policy and not to become involved in staff operations. Again, it should be emphasized that the relationship between the chief staff executive and individual directors, as well as the full board, must be clearly defined and adhered to.

The effective director will be knowledgeable of the affairs and activities of the association and will recognize the fiscal and legal responsibilities of the board and the individual directors. But the most important role of the director will be to ensure that the association assesses the needs of its members and of the industry, profession, or institutions it serves and develops a plan for the future which the association can follow even though the top leadership changes each year.

At times this planning may be difficult due to uncertainty regarding external factors which have an impact on the association. It will be difficult to establish specific objectives necessary to ensure that the plans for the future are achieved. But the director must view the development and approval of sound short-range and long-range objectives as one of the most important policy decisions he or she will be called upon to make. It is against these objectives that the board can review program progress and actually measure the effectiveness of the association in accomplishing its purpose.

In many instances directors will not have all the information they desire in order to make a decision and may be inclined to postpone it or assign it to a special committee or task force for further study. This step only fuels the proliferation of committees and delays progress. At times such as these the director must exercise decisive administrative and leadership ability in order to set a course of action for the association. It is these crucial decisions which usually mark the difference between a dynamic and growing association and a stagnant association.

The critical evaluation of the association's performance is the other major responsibility of the director. The good director will demand that the association's leadership take an objective look at its own achievements and at the effectiveness of the chief staff executive. The objectives set by the board should provide the primary basis for this evaluation.

A model position description for the board director is provided at the end of this chapter.

Role of Committees

As an association grows in size and complexity, the board is faced with an increasingly heavy workload. To ensure effective association performance and board direction, most associations find it necessary to establish committees of the board, and in some cases of the membership, to assist in developing relevant policies as well as in implementing policies, programs, and professional activities.

There is usually a small number of standing committees that are necessary to carry out the ongoing functions of the association. They are:

- **Executive Committee.** This committee usually possesses the authority and responsibility of the board of directors between meetings of the board in order to enable the association to respond quickly. Traditionally, the executive committee counsels the president or chairman. In some cases, it coordinates the work for all board committees and handles all matters that are not the specific responsibility of any other committees. The executive committee may also review recommendations from other committees before they are presented to the full board for action. The membership of the executive committee is usually composed of the officers of the association. The chief staff executive may be an ex officio member of the committee.
- **Finance Committee.** The finance committee is traditionally responsible for establishing the association's financial objectives and policies with approval of the full board. It reviews and approves the capital and operating budgets before they are submitted to the executive committee or board for approval and regularly monitors and approves financial statements to ensure that a sound fiscal posture is maintained. In some associations the finance committee is responsible for the investment of all funds.
- **Planning Committee.** This committee is usually responsible for long-range planning for the association and establishes goals and objectives for the future with assistance from the staff and approval of the board.
- **Membership Committee.** The membership committee traditionally has responsibility for maintaining the membership requirements of the association. In most cases, the membership committee is also responsible for working with the association staff to develop and support programs for membership recruitment.
- **Program or Education Committee.** This committee is usually concerned with recommending policies and objectives for educational

programs or other services that are provided to members. In some associations this committee or its subcommittee is responsible for planning the program for the annual meeting, convention, or symposium.
- **Publications Committee.** In some associations where this committee exists, it is responsible for setting editorial policies and for monitoring the publications program of the association. In some cases, its members may be responsible for reviewing manuscripts that are published in association journals or books. The publications committee frequently develops and recommends ideas for new publications.
- **Government Relations Committee.** The government relations committee is responsible for setting policies to guide the association's government relations activities and for working with the chief staff executive and other appropriate staff members to identify relevant political issues and develop strategies to address them. Members of the committee are frequently involved in making visits to Capitol Hill or their state legislatures and may testify before government bodies on behalf of the association.
- **Nominations Committee.** Traditionally, this committee is responsible for nominating members to run for office in the association.

The assignment of specific areas of responsibility to standing committees helps the board to clarify and strengthen its efforts to establish sound policies to guide the association's operations and to ensure evaluation of results. As a general guideline, the standing committee structure is intended to cover all major areas of planning and operation that require policies. Each association must determine the type and number of standing committees it requires.

There is often a proliferation of committees in associations. As a rule, associations should limit the number of standing committees. There is a tendency to establish a new standing committee to handle each new issue which arises. Instead, the responsibility should be assigned to an ad hoc committee or a special task force which has a specific charge and a timetable for accomplishing it. Unfortunately, some associations also use committee appointments to reward volunteer service, creating the requirement for additional committees that often lack purpose and objectives.

The effectiveness of committees depends on a number of factors:
- The degree to which the board sets objectives for committees or instructs them to act and the degree to which it monitors committee progress;
- The degree to which the chief staff executive works to motivate the committees and support them with staff work; and
- The performance of the committee chairman and the individual committee members.

The committee chairmen are usually appointed by the chief elected officer of an association. The role of the committee chairman is to direct the members and activities of the committee to see that it fulfills its responsibilities. The effective chairman:

- Ensures that the committee has specific objectives for the year whether they are set by the board or president or by the committee itself;
- Ensures that individual committee members understand committee objectives and their contribution to committee activities in order to achieve those objectives;
- Monitors committee member assignments;
- Prepares action-oriented agenda for meetings and ensures that committee members receive all relevant information or materials in time to prepare for the meetings;
- Directs meetings to ensure that important issues are discussed, resolutions are reached, and recommendations are developed when appropriate;
- Motivates and encourages committee members; and
- Helps to identify leadership talent.

A model position description for the committee chairman is presented at the end of this chapter.

The chairman and the committee are only as effective as the individual committee members. In some associations, the president or chairman appoints committee members; in others the chairman has the responsibility to select the committee members. Regardless, the committee members should be chosen on the basis of their knowledge and experience in the area of the committee's assigned responsibilities.

The effective committee member will endeavor to understand and support the achievement of committee objectives, become knowledgeable in the area in which the committee has responsibility, be willing to make decisions when called upon to do so, take into consideration the interests of the association as a whole and avoid following personal interests or biases, attend meetings, and carry out committee assignments. A model position description for the committee member is included at the end of this chapter.

Weaknesses in Leadership Performance

Associations have not always utilized their volunteer resources effectively. As a result, association leadership may not adequately fulfill the roles and responsibilities that have been described. Traditionally, associations have not done a good job of developing their leaders. As already noted, orientation for new leaders is frequently inadequate; many associations fail to clearly define and communicate the responsibilities of volunteer leaders. The result is often weakness in leadership performance. Common examples are:

- **The board does not develop long-range plans for the association.** Consequently, there are no long-term objectives to guide committees and the professional staff in carrying out their responsibilities. In some cases, the membership may lose confidence in the association's ability to anticipate and respond to its needs and may question the value of membership.
- **Program priorities may change radically from year to year.** Without a clear understanding of the board's responsibility to chart a balanced future course and provide continuity for the association, and without a plan to guide them, new chief elected officers and board members may introduce conflicting programs and new directions each year. The result may be ineffectiveness and chaos within the association.
- **Committees proliferate and are ineffective.** If there is confusion about the direction of the association and constant change in programs, committees inevitably proliferate as they are created to address new issues and develop new ideas. In this environment, their charges are usually unclear. Without clear objectives they may accomplish little for the association.
- **The board becomes involved in internal operations.** If board members do not understand the board's role to set policy and the professional staff's responsibility to implement it, the board may become involved in internal operations. The frequent result is that the board neglects some of its responsibilities, interferes with the effective performance of the staff and may undermine the chief staff executive.
- **The board becomes immersed in budgetary details.** Without clear objectives and priorities the board does not have a good basis for evaluating proposed expenditures in terms of their possible contribution to the achievement of the association's purpose. As a result board members tend to focus on line items in the budget: specific salaries, individual workshop costs, etc., and may become immersed in details without determining the overall appropriateness of the budget.
- **Board meetings are not productive.** If the board does not focus on substantive issues and setting policy for the association, board meetings tend to be devoted only to information exchange and socializing. Such meetings do not make the most effective use of board members' valuable time.

Guidelines for Improving Leadership

There are numerous theories about leadership and ways to improve leadership performance. But given the weaknesses that are frequently evident in association leadership there are some general guidelines that are particularly relevant.

- **The association should identify and develop potential leaders.** The association should identify new, young members who appear to have leadership qualities and abilities and nurture them to become future leaders. There should be a process to guide them through the association hierarchy to ensure they gain the experience they will need to serve effectively in top leadership positions.

  Ideally, through this process the future leaders will develop good insights into diverse membership needs and understand the requirement to balance them for the good of the association as a whole. And if the development program is effective, they will learn the value, responsibility, and principles of leadership and recognize the distinctions between the role of the volunteers and the role of the professional staff.

- **The association should provide an effective orientation program for new board members.** Whether or not the association uses the leadership development program described above, the association should orient new board members to prepare them for their leadership roles. The orientation program should be held each year, preferably at the association's headquarters, prior to the time new directors assume office.

  The orientation program should include a formal workshop that includes presentations by key members of the professional staff on the functions and responsibilities of the headquarters' organization. The presentations and accompanying briefing materials should cover: association goals and objectives and a five-year plan if one exists; responsibilities of the board director; responsibilities of committees and committee members; existing board and association policies; recent board decisions; and a discussion of the major issues facing the association and its members. If possible the program should also address governance and management principles that are relevant to the director's role and responsibilities.

- **The board should adopt an operating philosophy.** The board should have an operating philosophy to guide its actions throughout the year. Each year the board should review the previous philosophy and adopt it or revise it to meet its needs. The purpose of this philosophy is to clearly set forth the manner in which the board will operate and to clarify the working relationship between the board members and the president or chairman.

- **The board should maintain at least a five-year plan for the association.** If the association does not have a five-year plan, the board must first develop one with the assistance of the chief staff executive and other professional staff members. Each year thereafter, the board should review the plan in light of external and internal changes and update it as appropriate.

- **The board should set annual objectives to guide its activities.** The board should have objectives that determine what it will accomplish during the year. These objectives may be derived directly from the five-year plan for the association or they may be more specifically related to board actions. Regardless, they should be consistent with the objectives set forth in the five-year plan.
- **The board should maintain a board policy manual.** The board should maintain an up-to-date manual that includes all board policies and operating procedures. Each time a new policy or procedure is adopted or an existing one is revised, the manual should be updated. This manual will serve as a reference to guide the board in its actions.
- **The board should follow an action-oriented docket system for its meetings.** This system is designed to make the most productive use of the board members' limited time. The requirements of the system are:
  - All actions brought before the board should be clearly identified as either an action or an information item. All action items should be documented fully and should contain specific recommendations for action. The supporting data should note the attitude, approval, opinion or concurrence of others who should have reviewed and analyzed the problem (for example, committee members).
  - Except in emergency situations, no issue should be considered by the board unless it has been placed on the meeting agenda beforehand.
  - The agenda and its supporting data should be sent to each director sufficiently in advance of the meeting to allow time for preparation.
  - Actions by the board should be decisive, whether the action taken concerns rejection of a recommended policy, modification of a policy, request for additional data on which to base an opinion, or referral for review to the appropriate committee of the board.
  - The agenda and supporting information should be contained in a bound docket. The information should be separated according to major functional areas of activity, perhaps coinciding with the committees of the board. Following each item requiring an action, space should be provided for the director to note questions to raise at the meeting, to recast a resolution, or simply to write comments.

POSITION DESCRIPTIONS FOR VOLUNTEER LEADERS

POSITION TITLE: President or Chairman of the Board

BASIC FUNCTION:

Serves as chief elected officer of the association, representing the entire membership. Directs other officers, presides as chairman over board actions and may act as chief spokesman for the association.

SPECIFIC RESPONSIBILITIES:

1. Presides at all meetings of the association's board of directors and executive committee.

2. Schedules and prepares the agenda for meetings of the board of directors and executive committee.

3. Keeps the board of directors, executive committee, and association committees informed on the conditions and operations of the association.

4. Selects or approves chairmen for all association committees and task forces. Outlines the purposes and duties of the committees and monitors their progress.

5. Directs the board of directors in formulating policies and programs that will further the goals and objectives of the association.

6. Conducts an annual review of organizational performance and effectiveness, including a review of the chief staff executive's performance. When necessary, recommends changes in association structure (board, committees, etc.) to the board of directors.

7. May act as a spokesman for the association to the public, press, legislative bodies, and other related organizations. (In most associations this responsibility is shared with the chief staff executive. In others, the chief staff executive may have primary responsibility for these duties.)

8. Monitors association expenditures to assure operation within the annual budget. Provides for an independent annual audit of association finances.

9. Promotes active participation in the association on the part of the membership. May report the activities of the board and association to the members by newsletter or other regularly issued publication.

10. Presents an association report at the annual meeting.

POSITION TITLE: President-Elect or Chairman-Elect or Vice President or Vice Chairman

BASIC FUNCTION:

Assumes the responsibilities of the chief elected officer in his or her absence. Assists the chief elected officer in carrying out the functions of that office and performs specific duties delegated by the chief elected officer. This position may be used as an orientation for the future chief elected officer (especially in associations where there is automatic succession).

SPECIFIC RESPONSIBILITIES:

1. Assumes the duties of the chief elected officer in his or her absence.
2. Serves as a member of the board of directors and the executive committee.
3. Performs duties assigned by the chief elected officer which may include serving as chairman of one or more of the association committees.
4. Assists the chief elected officer in the performance of his or her duties, whenever requested to do so.
5. Attends annual meeting and special meetings as directed by the chief elected officer.
6. Represents the association with other associations or organizations as requested by the chief elected officer.

POSITION TITLE: Secretary

BASIC FUNCTION:

Ensures that records are maintained of all association, board, and executive committee meetings. Serves on the board of directors and the executive committee.

SPECIFIC RESPONSIBILITIES:

1. Serves as a member of the board of directors and the executive committee.
2. May serve as chairman of one or more association committees, if requested by the chief elected officer.
3. Ascertains that records are maintained for all meetings of the association, the board of directors, and the executive committee.
4. Ensures that copies of the minutes of each meeting are provided to the chief elected officer and other officers and directors as appropriate.
5. Maintains current copies of the association rules and by-laws for use by the chief elected officer and the board of directors.
6. Performs other duties as may be assigned by the chief elected officer.

POSITION TITLE: Treasurer

BASIC FUNCTION:

Ensures the integrity of the fiscal affairs of the association. Serves on the board of directors, the executive committee, and usually the finance or budget committee.

SPECIFIC RESPONSIBILITIES:

1. Serves as a member of the board of directors, the executive committee, and the budget or finance committee.
2. Ensures that the association maintains accurate financial records.
3. Reviews association expenditures and financial status on a regular basis to ensure overall fiscal integrity.
4. Ensures that regular financial reports are submitted to the board of directors and executive committee and presents an annual financial report to the membership.
5. Submits the financial accounts of the association to an annual independent audit.
6. Performs other duties assigned by the chief elected officer, which may include serving as chairman of one or more committees.
7. Represents the association with other associations in organizations as assigned by the chief elected officer.

POSITION TITLE: Committee Chairman

BASIC FUNCTION:

Directs the members and activities of the committee to ensure that it meets its goals and objectives.

SPECIFIC RESPONSIBILITIES:

1. Assists in developing the committee objectives.

2. Informs committee members of objectives and their expected individual contributions and responsibilities.

3. Assists the chief elected officer in making committee member appointments.

4. Prepares meeting agendas and distributes relevant information to all members prior to the meeting.

5. Presides over committee meetings to ensure adherence to the major issues and purposes.

6. Assists the chief elected officer in identifying potential leaders among the committee members.

7. Encourages active participation by committee members in the activities of the association.

8. Prepares committee status reports for the board of directors.

POSITION TITLE: Committee Member

BASIC FUNCTION:

Attends all meetings of the committee, prepares committee assignments, and works toward the fulfillment of the committee objectives.

SPECIFIC RESPONSIBILITIES:

1. Attends all meetings of the committee.

2. Carries out individual assignments that are made by the committee chairman.

3. Reviews all relevant material prior to the committee meetings. Prepares to make contributions and voice objective opinions concerning the committee issues.

Chapter II

THE ROLE OF THE PROFESSIONAL STAFF

This chapter discusses the management challenge facing the professional staff of associations and provides an overview of the role and needs of the chief staff executive, staff specialists, and professional managers.

The Management Challenge

Managing the "third sector," as Peter Drucker has called our not-for-profit institutions and organizations—government agencies, colleges and universities, hospitals, and associations—is one of the major challenges of this century. Virtually every facet of our society, health care, education, and defense has been entrusted to one of these institutions. Consequently, as Drucker has stated: "The performance of modern society—if not the survival of each individual—increasingly depends on the performance of these institutions." [1]

During the past two decades, companies and professional groups have begun to rely more heavily on their associations to help them protect their interests and achieve their worthwhile goals. As a result, associations have a major impact on society. As the role of the association expands, the governing board expects more from the association's professional staff. For even though effective volunteer leadership is vital to the association, the professional staff is actually the key to its success.

---

[1] Drucker, Peter F., *People and Performance: The Best of Peter Drucker on Management*, Harper's College Press, 1977, p. 9.

The Challenge to Professional Staff

The role of your association staff is to implement the policies of the board, keep the members happy by meeting their needs, and do this within an annual budget of $12,400. (Guidance from an association president to a new chief staff officer—1925.)

Perhaps this basic definition of the association staff's role still applies: implement board policies, keep the members happy, and stay within the budget. But the challenges professional association managers face today in fulfilling this role are unprecedented.

Due to the growing complexity of modern society and the rapidly changing political, social, and economic conditions that affect associations, it will be increasingly difficult for boards to set clear-cut policies which the association staff needs for guidance. Also, it will be harder to satisfy members since they will expect more services, but resist increases in dues. This situation combined with spiraling inflation and attendant rising costs will mean that "staying within the budget" will be a great challenge for many associations.

Given all these factors, it will be critical that the chief staff executive work with the board to set specific objectives for the association. Without them there would be no guidelines for allocating financial and staff resources, or no basis for ensuring that all the professional staff are working toward common goals in support of the association's purpose.

If the board does not officially approve objectives for the association, the chief staff executive and other members of the professional staff will end up setting objectives through their activities and the decisions they make. The danger in this informal evolutionary process is that when the board realizes that it is not determining the future direction of the association, some of the members may feel the chief staff executive is exceeding his or her authority and undermining the board. This situation thus places the chief staff executive in an untenable position.

To respond to the members' increasing demands for more service and more specialized assistance, association staffs will inevitably grow and become more diverse. As new programs and new publications are added, for example, divisions or operating units generally expand vertically because more staff are needed. And to address complex and specialized issues, associations hire staff experts in government, public relations, economics, consumer affairs, and other areas.

With these larger staffs, division or unit directors will be expected to emphasize managerial skill more than the technical skill they have in their particular areas. They will be responsible for ensuring that their staffs are working efficiently and effectively, and that the work of the staff experts or specialists is integrated into the association program to support the association's goals and objectives. Also, managers will be expected to motivate and develop personnel in order to ensure that the association has a strong and capable staff that can provide the required expertise and continuity to support the growth of the association.

The diagram below illustrates the need for supervisors to focus more attention on managerial skills as they assume more responsibility. As the diagram shows, the higher the manager rises in the organization, the more time he or she should spend in planning, directing, and monitoring staff activities, and the less time actually performing technical duties.

SKILLS NEEDED BY ASSOCIATION STAFF

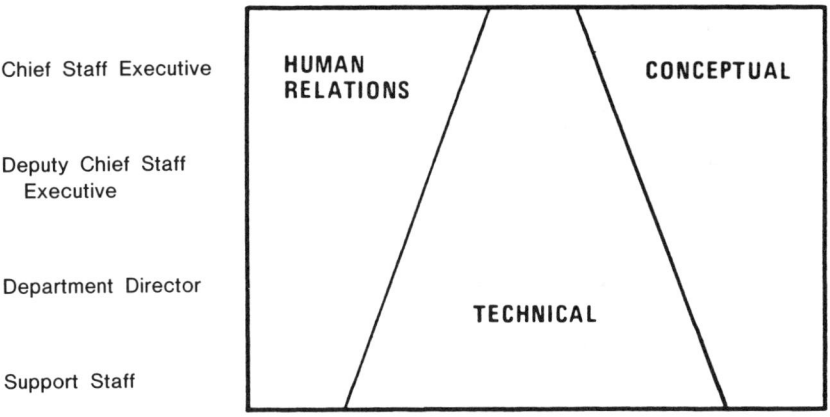

■ The lower the managerial position, the more technical skills needed.
■ The higher the managerial position, the less technical and more human relations and conceptual skills required.

In summary, as the professional staff grows, it will become a complex balance of diverse managerial, technical, clerical, and mechanical skills. All the staff will play different roles and have different needs. To ensure effective management and utilization of staff resources it is important to recognize these different roles and needs.

Overview of Professional Staff Roles and Needs

Specific functions and responsibilities of various association staff positions can be defined in position descriptions, but there are certain critical aspects of staff roles that should also be given special attention. All employees of an association have some basic professional needs that must be met if they are to be successful in carrying out their responsibilities.

The Chief Staff Executive

The ultimate measure of the chief staff executive's effectiveness is the overall performance of the association. The executive must be concerned about cost control, efficiency, and staff supervision, but in the final analysis results are the factor by which the association's performance is measured. Therefore, the association executive must manage for effectiveness. For this reason it is critical that the executive have:

- Clear guidance on the association's goals, objectives, and board-approved priorities; and
- A clear statement of the boundaries of the executive's authority and responsibility to implement the board's policies and priorities.

Without these guidelines the chief staff executive has no basis for making management decisions regarding programs, staff, and expenditure of financial resources. Also, there are no criteria for measuring the association's performance and therefore none for measuring the executive's effectiveness.

The chief staff executive has other professional needs that are important to his or her role in the association. These needs are depicted in *Exhibit II-A* on the following page, in the context of board needs, membership needs, and staff needs. They include a good internal management system and regular information on the progress the staff is making in implementing objectives and on the financial posture of the association. Obviously, the chief executive must have adequate financial and staff resources to carry out the work which has been assigned to the association. And, of equal importance, the freedom and authority to manage those resources. Finally, one of the most crucial needs of the chief staff executive is professional development. In light of the quickly changing environment and the requirements placed on the association, the chief executive must constantly upgrade his or her knowledge and abilities in order to respond effectively.

As do all staff, the chief staff executive needs an accurate, up-to-date position description that clearly sets forth the responsibilities of the job.

Staff Specialists

As already mentioned, as associations grow and their programs and activities become more complex, they usually have need for specialized assistance and hire professional level staff whose strengths are expertise and substantive knowledge in certain areas rather than management or supervisory abilities. Examples of these staff positions are the economist, the consumer affairs specialist, the advertising director, and the legal counsel or staff attorney. According to traditional organizational theory, the role of staff positions is to provide advice and counsel to the chief staff executive and other staff managers. As such, staff positions are assumed to be supplemental to the "line" organization which is responsible for execution of

Exhibit II-A ORGANIZATIONAL NEEDS IN WELL-MANAGED ASSOCIATIONS

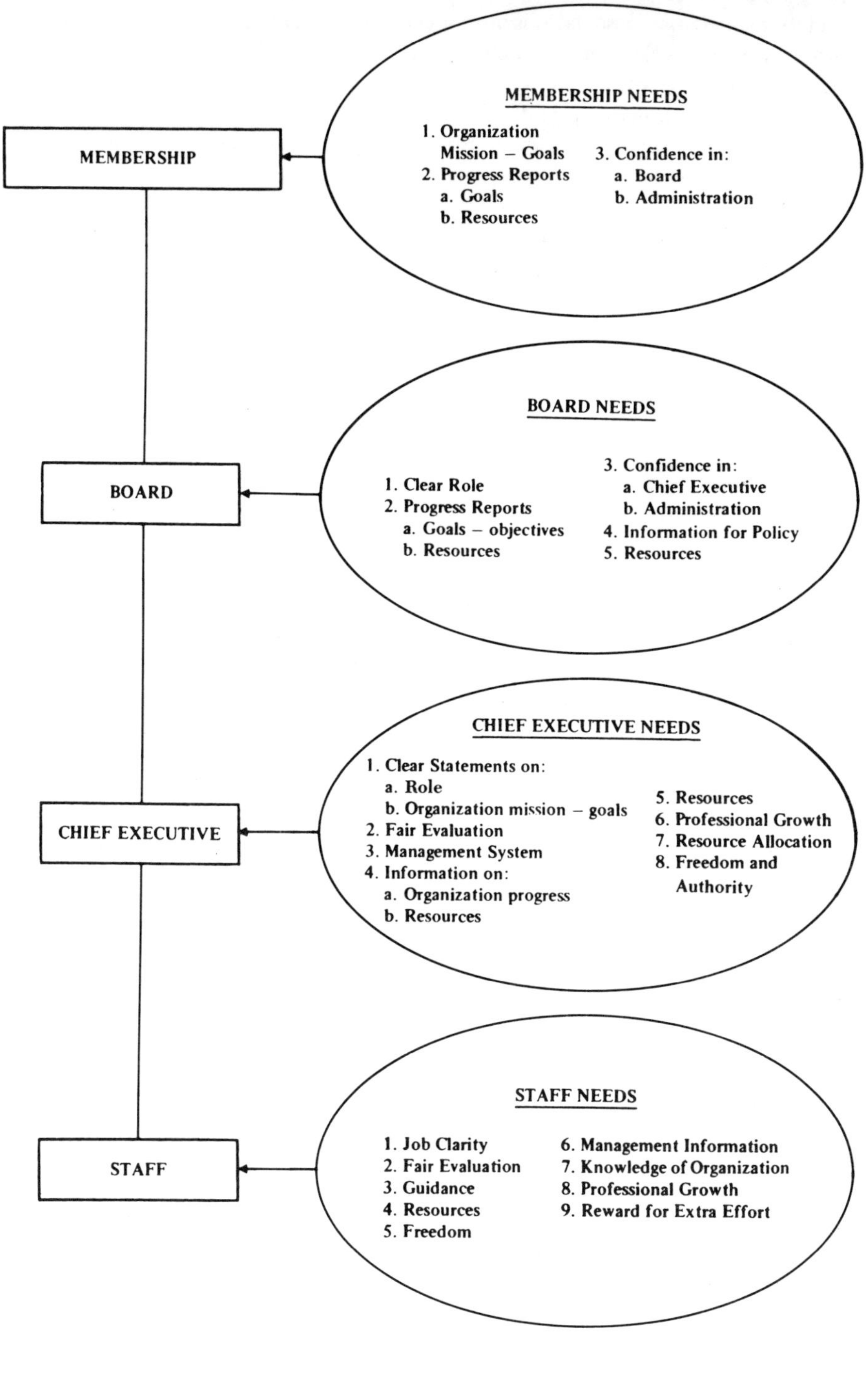

MEMBERSHIP ← **MEMBERSHIP NEEDS**
1. Organization Mission – Goals
2. Progress Reports
   a. Goals
   b. Resources
3. Confidence in:
   a. Board
   b. Administration

BOARD ← **BOARD NEEDS**
1. Clear Role
2. Progress Reports
   a. Goals – objectives
   b. Resources
3. Confidence in:
   a. Chief Executive
   b. Administration
4. Information for Policy
5. Resources

CHIEF EXECUTIVE ← **CHIEF EXECUTIVE NEEDS**
1. Clear Statements on:
   a. Role
   b. Organization mission – goals
2. Fair Evaluation
3. Management System
4. Information on:
   a. Organization progress
   b. Resources
5. Resources
6. Professional Growth
7. Resource Allocation
8. Freedom and Authority

STAFF ← **STAFF NEEDS**
1. Job Clarity
2. Fair Evaluation
3. Guidance
4. Resources
5. Freedom
6. Management Information
7. Knowledge of Organization
8. Professional Growth
9. Reward for Extra Effort

programs and services. But these distinctions are frequently blurred in associations because associations are service organizations. And, as a result, some of the positions mentioned as specialized "staff" areas may be considered "line" positions in some associations.

Generally, however, staff specialist positions may be considerably different from the typical line management positions—director of membership services or director of industry programs, for example. Although the staff specialist has the same staff needs—job clarity, fair evaluation, adequate resources, freedom of operation—shown in the diagram in Exhibit II-A, the types of professional growth opportunities are usually different.

As line managers progress upward in the organizational and management hierarchy, they need less technical ability and more human relations and conceptual skills. Unless the staff specialist supervises many other specialists, this requirement does not apply. In a role as counselor and advisor, the staff specialist must keep current and proficient in his or her area of expertise.

In most cases if the specialist fails to remain current the immediate negative consequences for the association may be far greater than if the line manager does not upgrade his skills, although the long-term implications may be reversed. The prudent chief staff executive or other supervisor of staff specialists will recognize the need for the specialists to upgrade their knowledge continually and will ensure that they remain professionally active and attend workshops, seminars and conferences where they can keep abreast of changes in their specialty areas.

Since staff specialists generally focus more attention on their narrow fields of expertise than on their contribution to association-wide objectives, the chief staff executive and the other top-level executives in the association should ensure that the specialists understand the organizational objectives and that they are included in regular staff meetings and are made to feel they are integral to the delivery of the association's services.

Sample position descriptions for a variety of staff specialist positions are included in Chapter IV.

Association Managers

Management has been defined as "getting things done through people." This definition is particularly apt to association management where effective use of staff resources is the key to success. Professional association executives and staff directors strive to manage staff to ensure that the outcome of an effort is greater than the sum of the resources put into it. To achieve this result, the managers must minimize organizational and staff weaknesses and maximize strengths.

The effectiveness of the recruitment, placement, development, and promotion of staff usually determines whether the association has the capacity to deliver the required services and achieve organizational objectives. Therefore, the managers need clear policies and procedures that set appropriate and equitable standards for these areas. Also, the assessment of staff capability must be based on factual evidence of performance against explicit objectives and requirements. As a result, managers need to understand the goals, objectives, and priorities of the association, as well as their responsibility and authority to attain them, in order to allocate staff resources effectively and determine their success in achieving the desired ends.

Once these requirements are met and there is a framework and supporting procedures for management, the role of the association managers—the vice presidents, directors, area managers—consists of:

- Organizing activities and dividing work tasks into management assignments;
- Communicating effectively to create a team from the various people who make up the organizational unit;
- Motivating the team and ensuring that the members understand how their individual and combined efforts help the association realize its goals; and
- Measuring the results of the team's efforts and the individual efforts and communicating the meaning of the measurements appropriately to the members.

The long-term growth of an association may depend, in large part, on the degree to which it develops its management staff. Therefore the association should ensure that it provides good professional development opportunities for its current or potential management personnel. To facilitate the development of these people, the association should have an effective performance appraisal system that identifies the managers' strengths and weaknesses in order to reinforce strong points and help address limitations.

Support Staff

Any staff member of an association needs the stability and direction provided by a clear authority structure. This requirement is particularly necessary for the wide variety of support staff that may be employed within the association. In addition, support staff must have productive work assignments. This point may seem axiomatic. But, in fact, a major cause of dissatisfaction among support staff is the absence of a sense of achievement or job fulfillment. Surprisingly, many positions are created and staffed without sufficient productive work to sustain them.

Like all employees, support staff also need regular and constructive feedback on their performance. The association should provide training and development opportunities for support staff in order to help them address weaknesses, once they are identified, and to help them grow in their positions.

Chapter III

ORGANIZATION FOR MANAGEMENT

This chapter briefly discusses the evolution of organizational structures within associations and societies, sets forth principles of association management that should be used as a guide in developing a structure, discusses the use of organization charts and methods for developing them, and presents some alternate forms of organizational structure for the management of associations and professional societies.

Evolution of Organizational Structures

Through the decades, associations have played a vital and worthwhile role in society, whether their purpose was to meet the needs of a group of companies or to provide services to professionals in an allied field. If the association is meeting the needs of its members, it inevitably expands its range of services and grows in size and stature as the industry or profession grows. The challenge is to ensure that services and programs keep pace with the needs of the membership; for, as the table on the next page indicates, the basic purpose of an association is to deliver services to its members or constituents.

This purpose is difficult to accomplish and its achievement often presents a major challenge for the association executive. For, in fact, the effective management and direction of an association is one of the most challenging jobs in the field of management. The responsibilities and requirements of the position are widely diverse. The chief staff executive must be an astute manager, able to organize the association's resources to ensure the most efficient delivery of services in order to satisfy the changing needs

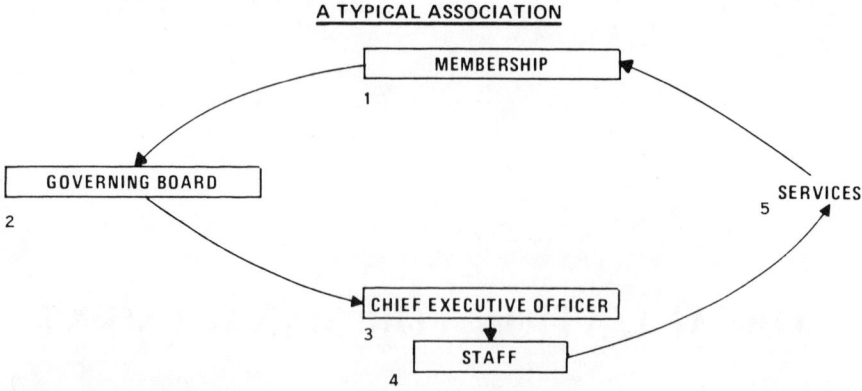

of the membership. In addition, the executive is often expected to expand services while avoiding a dues increase, a task that requires sound financial and business acumen. The chief staff executive must be a consummate politician and, at times, even a soothsayer. Given these demands, it is not surprising that some executives have described the post of chief staff executive as an "unmanageable position."

The success with which a chief staff executive carries out the responsibilities of the position are dictated in large measure by the effectiveness of the internal staff organization. Unfortunately, one of the major deficiencies in association management is the failure of chief staff executives to plan and organize for effective internal administration. Instead, they permit the organization to evolve rather than actively taking charge of the structure to decide how functions will be organized and to determine what types of knowledge and ability are required to direct the functional units. Not surprisingly, given the combination of rapid growth and the evolutionary nature of many associations, few organization structures are deliberately planned. As a result, many associations grow without structure or direction. As new functions emerge, they are often simply assigned to existing staff as collateral duties. Yet, the chief staff executive and the board are still frequently surprised when some positions become overburdened and things begin to "drop through the cracks," or the entire structure becomes unwieldy.

While this situation may be hard to fathom for someone who has not been in association management or enjoyed the experience of starting a new association and nurturing its growth, it becomes easier to understand if one looks at the traditional development process of associations. The first chief staff executive is often a person working part-time to meet the special needs of a small number of members. If the incumbent of that position carries out the responsibilities well and there is, in fact, a need for the association, membership begins to grow along with demands for services. The board decides it is time for a full-time chief administrative officer—and then another employee, and another and yet another. After a ten- to fifteen-year period, the "small association" may find itself with 50 employees and an operating budget in excess of $2 million. Sometimes, the same founding executive still heads the association. If so, that executive has learned how to apply the principles of association management, has developed a sound organizational structure, and is an effective association executive.

By this time, many association executives have found that a management by objectives process helps them handle a growing and increasingly diverse organization. They work with the staff directors and staff specialists to evolve specific annual objectives, workplans, and budgets. The staff is then responsible for the achievement of those objectives within the established time frames and budgets. Through regular monitoring of progress toward achievement of the objectives, the chief staff executive is able to maintain control over a wide range of programs and activities and still have time to fulfill other executive responsibilities.

Unfortunately, too often the incumbents of these positions react to membership pressures for new services without logically and systematically analyzing how the programs will be absorbed into the association. The resulting organizational structure frequently appears as if it has been designed by a committee. But there are principles of organizational management that successful associations have applied, and, if these guidelines are followed, they help to ensure that an organization is properly structured and staffed.

Obviously, no single organizational structure can be taken off the shelf and applied without adapting it to the unique needs of the association. While an organizational structure will change as the association grows, if the principles of organizational management are followed, there is a good chance that the services to the membership will not be interrupted—nor will the tenure of the chief staff officer.

Principles of Organization

Organizing for the management of an association involves the systematic grouping of interdependent functions to form a unified structure. It is through this structure that authority, direction, coordination, and control are exercised in order to accomplish the objectives of the association. The organizational structure provides the framework within which the staff carry out their responsibilities. It represents a grouping of the human resources that must be coordinated in order for the association to achieve its purposes. Of all the areas of management, it is association management that most clearly requires recognition of the importance of human resources in applying organizational theory. The typical association does not rely on automated manufacturing processes or the efficient production of products to meet its goals and objectives; instead it depends on the effective management and utilization of staff to achieve its ends. For this reason, associations are perhaps the best example of the classical definition of management—

"getting work done through people." Accordingly, the organizational structure itself is nothing more than a diagram of reporting relationships, supported by operating policies and procedures. Until people are assigned to positions within the "blocks on the chart" and they begin to carry out their assigned responsibilities in an orderly and coordinated process, the structure has no meaning.

If we have learned anything in the past half century of applying organizational theory it is that there is no right or wrong organizational structure. The structure itself will be affected by many factors: the unique purposes of the organization, the needs of the members, the type of functions to be carried out, the size of the staff requried to perform the association functions, the role of the volunteers in delivering services to the membership, and the number of field offices or local chapters and their relationship to headquarters. Consequently, in considering the principles for organizing an association it is important to remember the need for practicality and flexibility.

The organizational principles that apply to virtually all associations are thus limited, but they are nonetheless of crucial importance. They are as follows:

- The board of directors or trustees of an association is responsible for approving policies and setting future directions. Therefore, the association's organizational framework must be structured to facilitate the formulation of policies by ensuring that the board has the information it needs to reach rational and sound decisions, and to support the execution of those policies through the day-to-day operations of the association.
- The chief staff executive of the association must have sole responsibility and adequate staff capacity for the achievement of the association's objectives and implementation of policies approved by the board.
- Similar and related functions should be combined or grouped to promote coordination and effective utilization of staff resources.
- Lines of supervisory control and areas of responsibility should be clearly defined.
- No person should be responsible in a line capacity to more than one supervisor.
- Each executive and each line supervisor should have full control over all personnel who carry out the work for which the supervisor is responsible. The supervisor should be accountable for the results.
- The span of control of the individual supervisor should not be exceeded. (Span of control is the number of support groups to which a single executive can give his or her time without exceeding the limits of effective attention.)

Regardless of the type of organizational structure that is developed and regardless of whether an association applies the recommended organizational principles, an organization chart should be developed. The following section discusses guidelines for developing an association's organization chart.

The Organization Chart

According to formal organization theory the association staff should be structured in the form of a triangle. The broad base of the triangle is composed of operating units supporting an ascending hierarchy of branches or divisions that forms the apex where a single executive exercises final authority over the association. The hierarchical pattern of organization is based on the theory that there is a limit to the number of support units that a single manager can effectively supervise. Hence, similar functions should be grouped wherever possible under a single manager so long as the span of control is not exceeded.

In addition, classical organization theory dictates that communications within the association proceed through "official channels." The larger the organization the more important these channels become. This formal communications process requires that an executive with certain rank or level in the hierarchy who has a need to communicate with an executive at a higher level in a different division must go up the chain of command or line of authority in his or her own division until an executive of rank equal to the one with whom he or she desires to communicate is reached; at this point the gap between the two divisions may be properly closed.

Obviously, in smaller organizations and, in fact, in many large organizations, the "proper" communication channels are frequently ignored or modified by agreement to allow flexibility. Common sense must always be a key factor in making an organizational structure work. Consequently, while the chart depicts a formal organizational structure, in most cases there is also an informal organizational structure underneath. Although the formal organizational chart depicts a desirable set of relationships within the organization, the "social" structure under which the staff actually operates is frequently quite different. In actuality relationships are often bypassed when staff find it more effective to work directly with the responsible person irrespective of the channels shown on the chart. Sometimes, decisions can be made or problems resolved more quickly during brief discussions in the staff lounge than they can in the formal surroundings of an office.

Thus, to the extent feasible, the chief staff executive of an association is well advised to attempt to assess the informal organizational structure and working relationships and take them into account before evolving and charting the formal organization for management of the association. Consistent with the theory of "social management" the informal structure should, if possible, guide the development of the formal chart. With this important caveat, some basic guidelines for developing association organizational charts are presented below:

- **Clarify the distribution of functional responsibilities.** An organization chart's most frequent use is as a reference source to identify the appropriate office or staff member to handle a specific task. Responsibilities should be explicit in every unit, allowing employees to determine what the rest of their colleagues actually do. In realizing the duties handled by other parts of the staff, employees come to understand what responsibilities they themselves are supposed to undertake. Good organization charts eliminate a "pass-the-buck" mentality among professional staff. They can be important motivational factors, emphasizing the importance of teamwork to the overall delivery of effective service. The chart generates familiarity, encouraging employees to contact the appropriate counterpart for expeditious completion of a task.
- **Whenever possible, incorporate all employees.** A fundamental mistake in many organizational efforts is the concentration upon managerial or professional positions. As a result, the chart is useful to only a portion of the association staff. Clerical or technical staff will pay less attention to an exhibit where their responsibilities are not outlined. If the chart is to be a comprehensive management tool, it should incorporate all staff functions. If an association staff is just too large to include on a single chart, there should be a set of charts for each major department. A sample of this type of chart is shown in *Exhibit III-A* on the following page.
- **Specify reporting responsibilities.** The lines of authority are a basic element to any position. In associations, they are all the more important if employees are to understand that they are accountable to the membership via the staff hierarchy. Clear supervisory relationships are essential to ensure general management control and to avoid any separate allegiances to factions within the association. The parameters of any position are strongly determined by who an employee will supervise and who, in turn, will supervise him or her. Unclear reporting responsibilities can be the cause of serious "turf battles" and job dissatisfaction. Be sure that employees at all levels understand who reports to whom.
- **Let the position titles reflect staff operations.** Organization charts are effective only as long as they are accurate. Be sure that each person on the chart is described by function as well as by title. Simply listing three directors hides a great deal of information about how the association operates. Identifying a director of public relations, a director of publications and a director of business services make the chart a more viable tool and reference guide. If an employee is wearing two hats, show the name twice on the chart. If an employee is

Organization for Management 39

Exhibit III-A

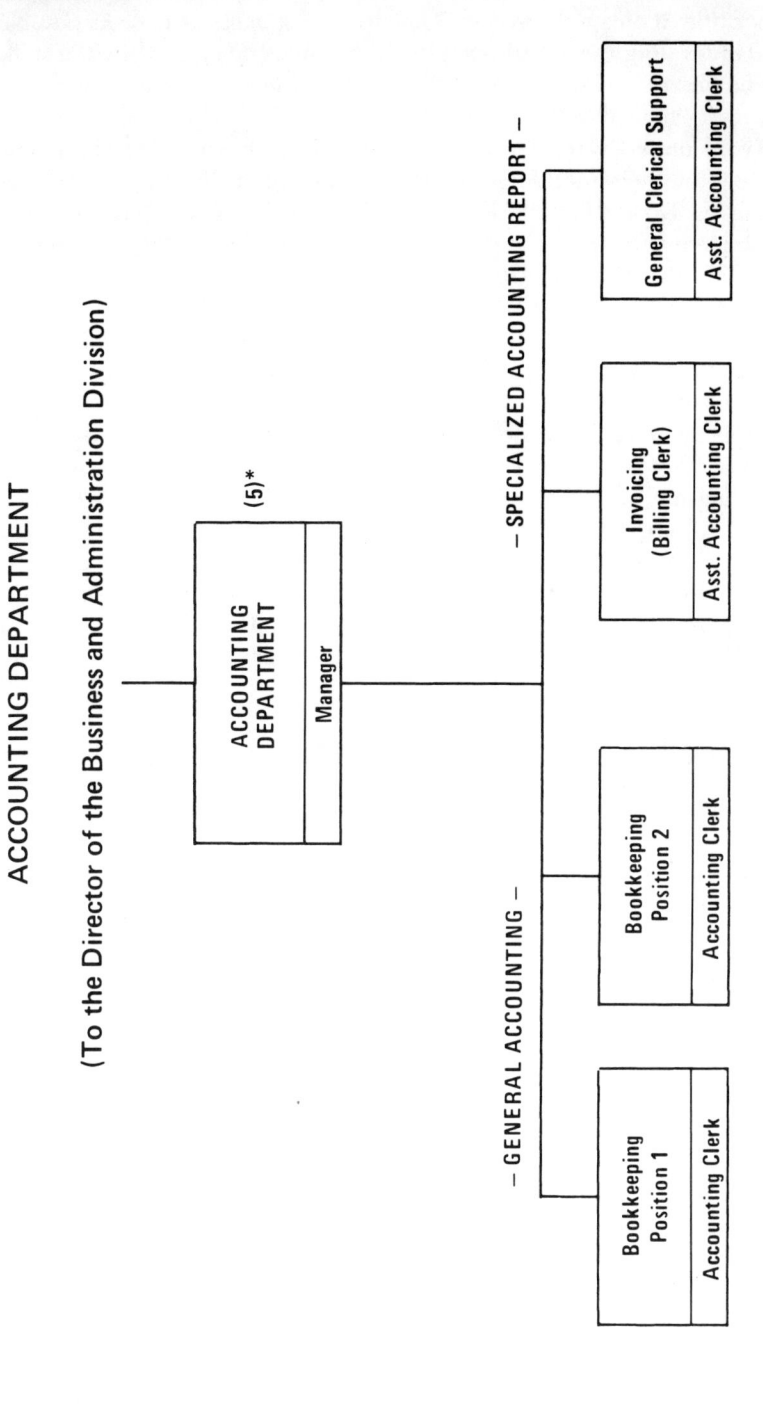

ACCOUNTING DEPARTMENT

(To the Director of the Business and Administration Division)

```
                    ACCOUNTING          (5)*
                    DEPARTMENT
                    ─────────────
                    Manager
                         │
     ┌───────────────────┼───────────────────┐
     │                   │                   │
─ GENERAL ACCOUNTING ─      ─ SPECIALIZED ACCOUNTING REPORT ─
     │                   │         │                   │
┌─────────┐        ┌─────────┐  ┌─────────┐      ┌─────────────┐
│Bookkeeping│      │Bookkeeping│ │Invoicing│      │General Clerical│
│Position 1 │      │Position 2 │ │(Billing │      │Support         │
│           │      │           │ │ Clerk)  │      │                │
├─────────┤        ├─────────┤  ├─────────┤      ├─────────────┤
│Accounting│       │Accounting│  │Asst.     │     │Asst.           │
│Clerk     │       │Clerk     │  │Accounting│     │Accounting Clerk│
│          │       │          │  │Clerk     │     │                │
└─────────┘        └─────────┘  └─────────┘      └─────────────┘
```

*Denotes total staff complement assigned to the Accounting Department.

assuming responsibilities beyond those normally associated with his/her title, indicate it anyway. The chart must come as close as possible to illustrating the actual operating procedures being used by the staff. The chart should make intuitive sense to the association insider who knows "how things are actually run."
- **Avoid unnecessary layers of bureaucracy.** Organization charts lose much of their usefulness when they become a diagram of staff seniority. Do not let considerations of longevity or personal standing interfere with the delineation of actual operating authority. Separating a decision maker from the implementing staff with a deputy position is a classic problem. Establish deputies as on-line intermediaries only if they actually perform that function persistently. Distinguish executive assistants or special support personnel from on-line staff who have operational responsibilities.
- **Consider actual workload rather than artistic symmetry.** Many systems of organization suffer from a misplaced emphasis upon "balancing out" the organization chart. Diagrams should reflect the fact that different functions may require different levels of effort. One association may require several departments and dozens of staff experts to handle research and only a two-person office to administer membership records. Another may concentrate its staff resources in public relations and publications. Let the organization chart indicate this functional emphasis. Avoid the urge to distribute staff equally to each division.
- **Use the chart as an ongoing project tool.** As they undertake new activities and address new issues, effective associations let their organizational arrangements evolve to meet new challenges. When an association staff is pointed in new directions by its membership, the organization chart should be a focus of how resources can be marshalled to take on the effort. If the new activity is a large one, a major reorganization may be in order. If the existing organizations can accommodate the new emphasis, only some minor revisions might be expected. In any case, a good organization chart will be a focus of discussion whenever new ideas and new services are contemplated. In a dynamic association, that will happen often.

These basic guidelines should serve associations representing any size or type of membership, although organizational structures in associations do vary greatly. As noted earlier, most associations develop through an evolutionary process. The association's growth may be rapid or slow depending on the nature and size of the membership base. It may occur as a result of a conscious decision to expand or in response to outside challenges (such as government regulation) which affect the interests of the constituency served by the association and create demands for new services and new capacities and spur a growth in membership.

Other associations may have a basically fixed membership which has specific limited needs which can be met by its association. Usually those needs are government and public representation. These organizations frequently do not follow the typical evolutionary process of growth.

Evolution of Organizational Structures

There are four major phases in association development. Each of these phases and the related changes in organizational structure are discussed in this section. The organizational structures are presented as "typical" examples of structures in associations at these four phases of development. However, in actuality there is no "typical" association and there is no single right way to organize a particular type or size of association. The structures are offered as hypothetical models and are intended to illustrate reasonable approaches to organization under certain circumstances. Discussion of the evolutionary process is intended to identify some of the organizational problems that arise as the association grows and that trigger the need for reorganization. The four typical structures which will be discussed are:

- The "new" association with one to three employees;
- The "emerging" association with four to 10 employees;
- The "developing" association with 11 to 30 employees; and
- The "large" association with more than 30 employees.

For consistency, the organizational structures are developed on a functional basis. This type of organizational structure emphasizes the specialization of function or process within the association. Each process or major activity forms the basis for a separate division and all are integrated through the coordination of line officials at successive levels of hierarchy, e.g., division director, branch manager, office supervisor. In a given association, for example, the functions of publications development and production, business services, and professional and industrial programs may be organized into separate divisions.

Discussion of the four alternate organizational structures does not go below the divisional level. The structuring and organizing of functions below that level of management would be sufficiently arbitrary and artificial to render the charts useless. Their purpose is to give the association executive a general idea of changes that occur in the organizational structures at different levels of growth and development.

Typical New Association

The typical new association begins with one to three employees, and, as shown in *Exhibit III-B* on the following page, the chief administrative officer is responsible to a board for carrying out the day-to-day activities. When the association is new and has only one or two professional staff members, the volunteer committees play an important role in carrying out

Exhibit III-B

THE TYPICAL NEW ASSOCIATION
– ONE TO THREE EMPLOYEES –

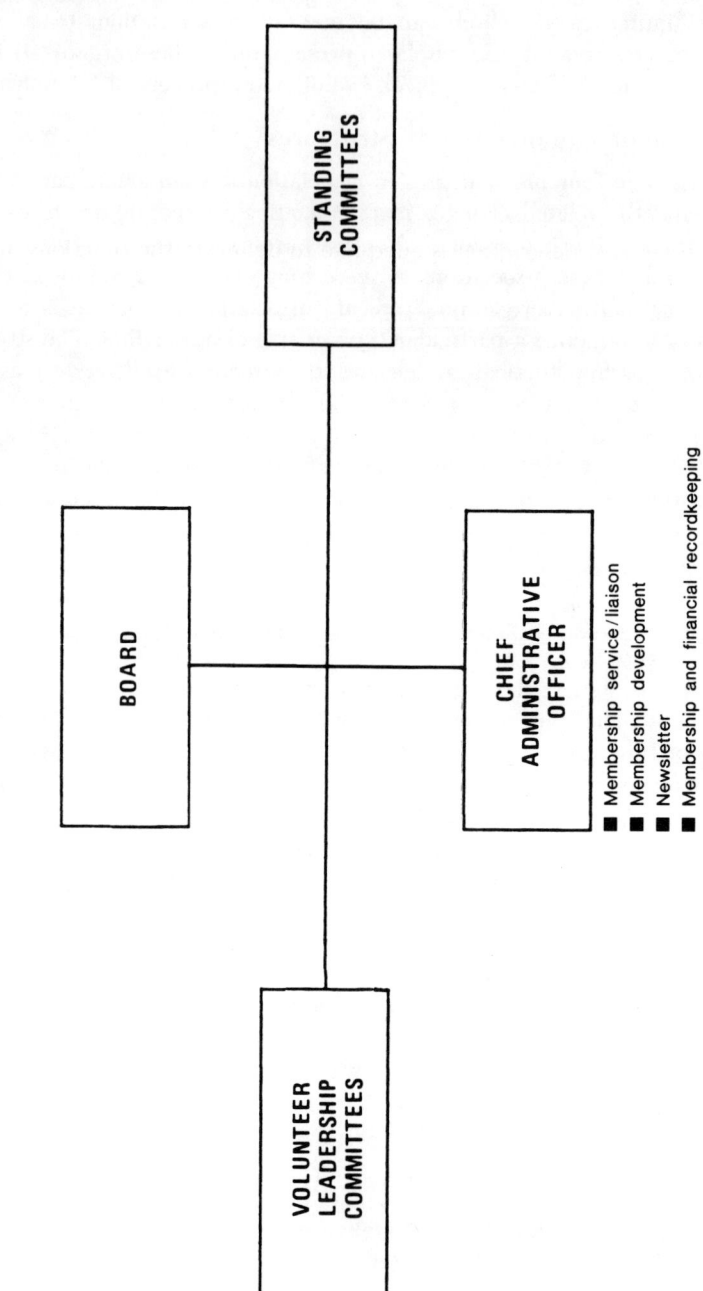

- BOARD
- STANDING COMMITTEES
- VOLUNTEER LEADERSHIP COMMITTEES
- CHIEF ADMINISTRATIVE OFFICER
  - ■ Membership service/liaison
  - ■ Membership development
  - ■ Newsletter
  - ■ Membership and financial recordkeeping
  - ■ Convention and meeting planning
  - ■ Government and public relations
  - ■ Supervision

the professional programming activities. These committees usually include an Executive Committee, Finance Committee, Membership Committee, Publications Committee, and an Education Committee. Instead of simply setting policies to guide these activities, the committees of the small new association are usually actively involved in the related functions.

Since the chief administrative officer is usually the only professional staff member of the association, a staff organization chart is really not needed to organize and establish the relationship of various functions. A thorough position description is adequate to delineate the functions that the chief administrative officer will carry out with assistance from one or two members of the support staff. Generally, the chief administrative officer is responsible for membership services and liaison with the membership as well as development of ideas and programs to increase membership. The membership responsibilities include recordkeeping and dues collection.

The next activity which is usually added in the new association is a publication program—typically consisting of a newsletter or some type of routine communication for the membership. Because there are no other professional staff, the chief administrative officer is usually responsible for writing copy and coordinating publication and distribution of the document. If a magazine or more extensive publication is developed at the outset, the volunteer leadership frequently makes a substantial contribution to the contents of the publication and retains editorial authority. In some instances a volunteer member may serve as editor or an outside editor and publishing company may be retained to handle the entire publication process.

Other typical responsibilities of the chief administrative officer in the small new association are coordination of arrangements for meetings and workshops and, in some cases, government and public relations activities. However, without additional staff there is a limitation to the scope of the activities the chief administrative officer can handle in these other areas.

If the chief administrative officer is able to function effectively in these diverse capacities and to help promote the services of the association to prospective members, the membership and programs of the organization grow. This growth is accompanied by expansion of the staff.

Typical Emerging Association

For this hypothetical discussion, the typical emerging association has four to ten full-time employees. The chief administrative officer begins to assume a different role and to have different responsibilities as additional staff is added to assume many of the routine functions described for the new association. Generally, the chief administrative officer now provides management oversight for staff carrying out many of the functions which he or she previously performed. However, the chief administrative officer usually retains immediate responsibilities for government relations since that activity frequently has major importance for associations. The chief administrative officer also continues to be responsible for financial management and external relations.

The other primary functions of the association in this size category can be divided into three logical groupings—publications, membership services, and business services. Staff below the executive level are hired to carry out these functions. As the organization chart for the typical emerging association (shown in *Exhibit III-C*) indicates, "coordinators" usually serve in these positions.

The coordinator in the publications area is responsible for the development and distribution of the newsletter as well as for providing some editorial support services if the association has a monthly or even quarterly journal. At this juncture of development the association usually does not have a full-time "editor," and a volunteer member continues to serve in that capacity, or the magazine or journal is published outside the association. There are exceptions depending on the nature and technical content of the publication. But generally in associations of this size, the publications coordinator is primarily responsible for editorial support rather than editorial control.

In this still relatively small association the membership coordinator's primary responsibility is membership recordkeeping. Working with the chief administrative officer, the membership coordinator also supports membership development activities. In many cases, the coordinator makes arrangements and provides support services for the association's annual meeting or convention and for board meetings, committee meetings, workshops, and seminars.

The administrative services and accounting requirements of the emerging association have grown sufficiently to warrant a full-charge bookkeeper. The bookkeeper also maintains records of accounts and personnel records, handles payroll, and purchases supplies.

In summary, the typical emerging association begins to consolidate similar functions and relies on the chief administrative officer to supervise other "professional" staff as well as continue to personally handle a number of important functions.

Typical Developing Association

For this discussion, the typical developing association has 11 to 30 employees. By this stage the association is "developing" into a multipurpose, full-service association which provides a relatively broad range of activities for its membership. The chief administrative officer now finds it necessary to assume greater managerial and leadership responsibilities and probably is better described as the "chief staff executive." The primary role of the chief officer is to provide overall management and direction for the activities and staff of the association, but the incumbent also usually retains responsibility for public outreach and external relations.

Exhibit III-C

THE TYPICAL EMERGING ASSOCIATION
— FOUR TO TEN EMPLOYEES —

```
                    VOLUNTEER
                    LEADERSHIP
                    COMMITTEES
                         |
                       BOARD ───────────── STANDING
                         |                 COMMITTEES
                         |
                    CHIEF
                    ADMINISTRATIVE
                    OFFICER
                    ■ General management
                    ■ Government relations
                    ■ Financial management
                    ■ Public relations
         ┌───────────────┼───────────────┐
    PUBLICATIONS    MEMBERSHIP        BUSINESS
                    SERVICES          SERVICES
    Coordinator     Coordinator       Bookkeeper
    ■ Newsletter,   ■ Membership      ■ Bookkeeping
      magazine        development     ■ Purchasing
    ■ Editorial     ■ Educational     ■ Liaison with C.P.A.
      support         programs        ■ Membership recordkeeping
      services      ■ Convention
    ■ Advertising     planning
                    ■ Membership
                      support services
```

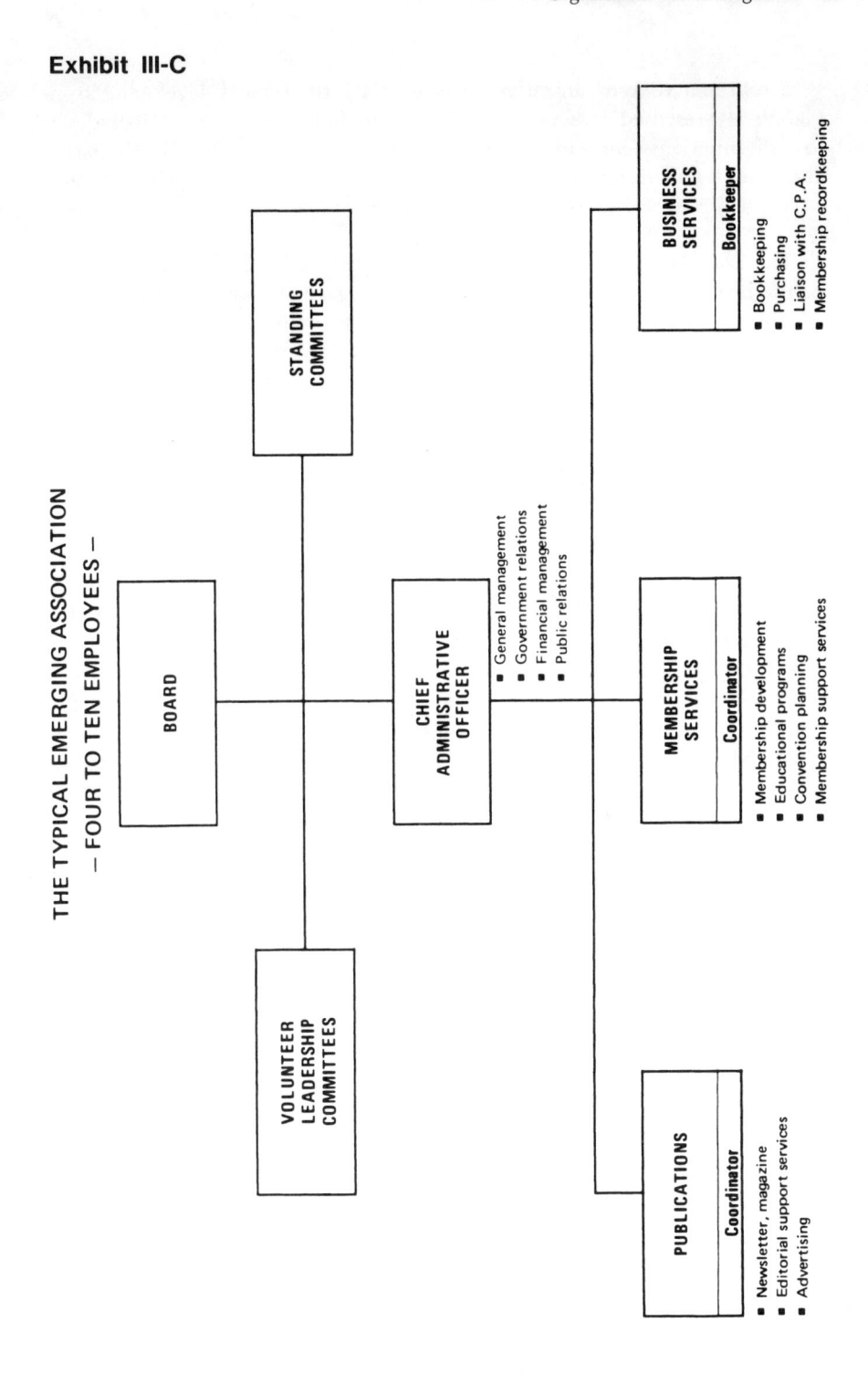

A representative organizational structure for the typical developing association is presented in *Exhibit III-D* on the following page. It includes two staff functions—an administrative assistant and a government relations coordinator—and three line organizations—a division of professional or industry programs, a division of publications, and a division of business services.

The placement of the staff functions on the table of organization indicates their day-to-day contact and supporting relationship to the chief staff executive. The administrative assistant's primary role is to provide direct support to the chief staff executive in fulfilling the responsibilities of his or her position. In that capacity the assistant assumes tasks of greater difficulty and complexity than those handled by an executive secretary. In addition, the administrative assistant frequently plays an important role in supporting the board of directors. The assistant normally attends board meetings, takes minutes, and oversees facilities and arrangements at the meetings.

The government relations coordinator also works closely with the chief staff executive; for although a position has been created to handle this function, it is usually sufficiently important to the association to warrant the executive's close attention. In some instances, if the association is not located in Washington, D.C., the government relations office is nevertheless a Washington office. In this case the head of the government relations office is likely to be a more senior person capable of executing the government relations program without day-to-day direction and guidance. On the other hand, in some associations government relations is not a critical function and therefore may not be assigned to a special office.

When there is a government relations office in the developing association, it maintains federal or state government contacts, answers inquiries regarding federal or state legislative and regulatory activities, prepares briefings for testimony before Congress or state legislatures, and disseminates information on legislative issues.

The remaining functions in the typical developing association can be grouped into three areas of sufficient size and complexity to warrant the assignment of a director to head them. Directors rather than coordinators usually fill these positions since the incumbents must possess stronger managerial abilities. As the association has grown from an emerging association to a developing association, the major functional units have grown vertically, adding programs and activities that require additional staff. In some cases, the directors may be responsible for supervision of as many as ten to twelve staff members. In addition to managerial ability, the directors must have substantive technical knowledge of the areas over which they have jurisdiction. At this stage of the association's evolution, the directors are typically the most technically knowledgeable people in the divisions. Each of the three typical line divisions are discussed in the remainder of this section.

Organization for Management 47

Exhibit III-D

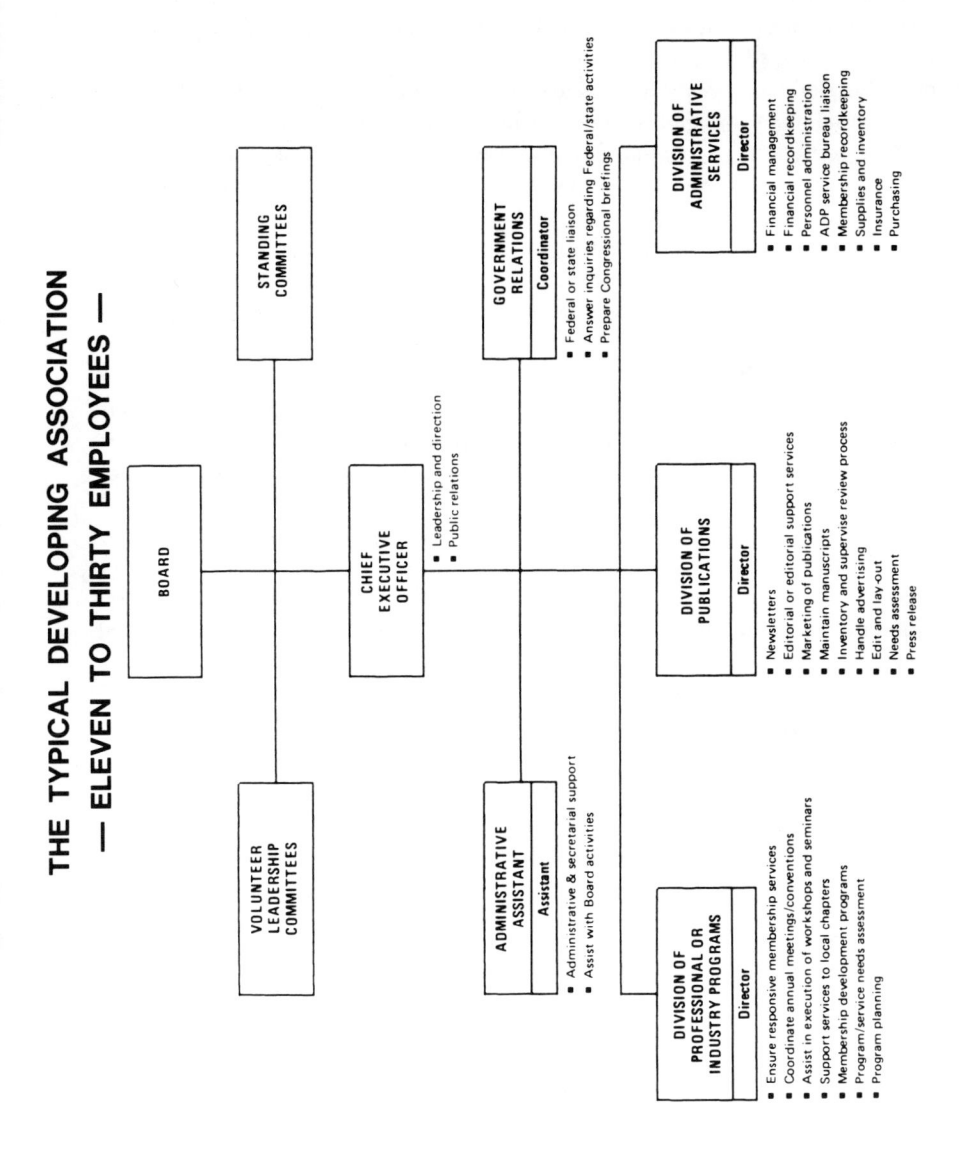

THE TYPICAL DEVELOPING ASSOCIATION
— ELEVEN TO THIRTY EMPLOYEES —

BOARD

VOLUNTEER LEADERSHIP COMMITTEES

STANDING COMMITTEES

CHIEF EXECUTIVE OFFICER
- Leadership and direction
- Public relations

ADMINISTRATIVE ASSISTANT
- Administrative & secretarial support
- Assist with Board activities

GOVERNMENT RELATIONS
Coordinator
- Federal or state liaison
- Answer inquiries regarding Federal/state activities
- Prepare Congressional briefings

DIVISION OF PROFESSIONAL OR INDUSTRY PROGRAMS
Director
- Ensure responsive membership services
- Coordinate annual meetings/conventions
- Assist in execution of workshops and seminars
- Support services to local chapters
- Membership development programs
- Program/service needs assessment
- Program planning

DIVISION OF PUBLICATIONS
Director
- Newsletters
- Editorial or editorial support services
- Marketing of publications
- Maintain manuscripts
- Inventory and supervise review process
- Handle advertising
- Edit and lay-out
- Needs assessment
- Press release

DIVISION OF ADMINISTRATIVE SERVICES
Director
- Financial management
- Financial recordkeeping
- Personnel administration
- ADP service bureau liaison
- Membership recordkeeping
- Supplies and inventory
- Insurance
- Purchasing

The *division of professional or industry programs* may, at this stage of the association's development, consolidate all membership services except publications. In most cases, the director of this division is responsible for ensuring that services are responsive to the needs of the membership, for assisting in the planning and execution of workshops and seminars, and for providing chapter support services. In addition, the division of professional or industrial services usually coordinates the planning and preparation for the annual meeting and markets exhibit space. However, in some developing associations, a convention and meeting coordinator may report directly to the chief staff executive in order to ensure that these important and highly visible events are carried out as smoothly as possible and that the exhibit space is marketed aggressively and effectively.

In addition, it is not unusual to find the membership development function assigned in this division. The staff of the division have the greatest contact with the members and are in the best position to observe their needs and identify programs and services that will attract new members as well as help to retain existing members. It should be noted that in some associations membership development may also be a staff function reporting directly to the chief staff executive when membership dues represents the major source of income for the organization.

In the developing association, the *division of publications* usually has a small staff that is responsible for developing the newsletter or newsletters, booklets, brochures, and other publications. The division continues to provide editorial and publication support services for the magazine or journal, including editing, lay-out, paste-up, and proofreading. However, it is also not unusual to find a full-time editor and even associate or assistant editors on the staff who have primary responsibility for the development of articles for the monthly or bimonthly journal. Further, in this stage of the association's development, the publications division is frequently concerned with the marketing of the publications and the solicitation of advertising in order to ensure a stream of revenue to fund the expansion of the publications program.

The *division of business services*, in the developing association, has increasing financial management responsibilities in addition to routine line item accounting and bookkeeping. The staff of the division has greater responsibility for managing the association's limited financial resources. Usually, greater emphasis is placed on the purchasing function—ordering in larger, yet lower unit cost quantities, developing better bidding procedures, and ensuring that the maximum coverage possible is obtained for each insurance dollar expended.

As the number of employees in the developing association increases, personnel administration becomes a more formal and complex function. Greater emphasis is placed on personnel management, affirmative action, and management of compensation and benefit programs. However, only in the largest developing associations is there likely to be a personnel officer who focuses solely on personnel matters.

As membership in the association grows, the membership recordkeeping function becomes increasingly complex and time-consuming. Therefore, the large developing associations are likely to use automatic data processing services or acquire their own computer system to process membership records. These changes in recordkeeping systems require the addition of staff with special knowledge and expertise.

Typical Large Association

Clearly, there is no "typical" large association, since that category encompasses a diverse group of associations, ranging in size from 30 employees to hundreds of employees. But there are some clear differences in organization and structure once the number of employees grows beyond 30. At this stage in the association's growth the chief paid officer is truly acting in an executive capacity. The chief staff executive provides overall management and leadership for the organization, plans for the future of the association and its constituency, and serves as spokesman for the association and, in many cases, for the profession or industry the association represents.

Exhibit III-E on the following pages shows the complex structure of staff and activities the chief staff executive of the association must manage effectively to ensure that the purpose and objectives of the association are met. Although the position is not shown on the organization chart, some associations hire a deputy chief staff executive to support the chief executive. As the table of organization indicates, the complexity and diversity of the chief executive's responsibilities require that top level staff support be provided in critical areas such as government relations and public relations. In addition, although not shown on the chart, there is often an administrative assistant and, in some cases, special assistants to the chief executive in areas of importance to the association.

The large association generally has diverse publics which it must serve, interact with, keep informed, and influence. For this reason, the public relations function requires a person of "director" level caliber and experience to provide direction as well as specialized expertise in order to ensure that an effective public relations program is maintained. The office of public relations is responsible for planning and executing a public relations strategy, maintaining contacts with the media, preparing press releases, press kits, brochures, and related materials, arranging press conferences, and writing speeches in some subject areas.

The office of government relations in the large association is usually responsible for a multifaceted government affairs program. The program always involves achieving recognition and maintaining good will among federal or, if appropriate, state legislatures, and government agencies. De-

Exhibit III-E

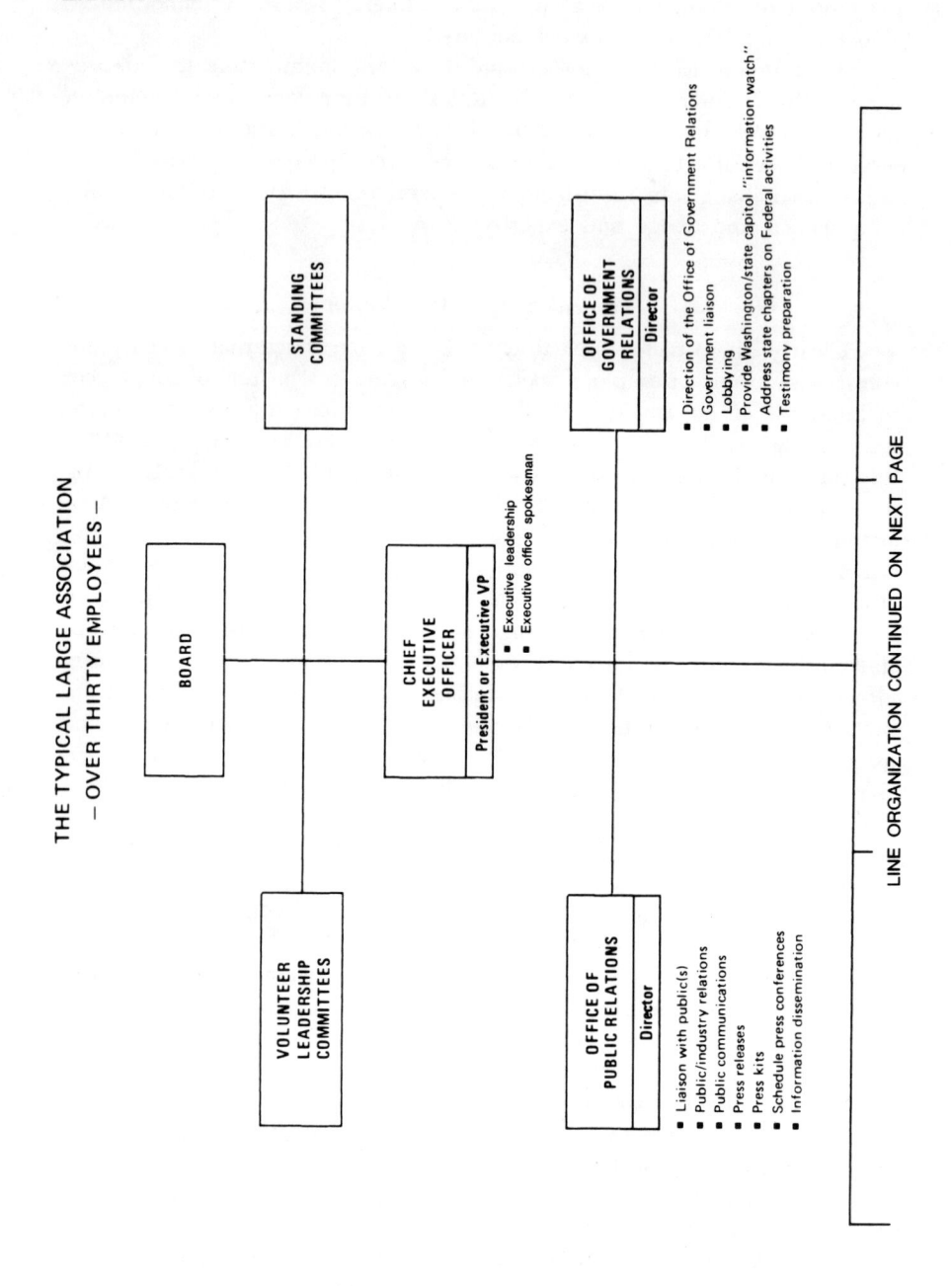

THE TYPICAL LARGE ASSOCIATION
— OVER THIRTY EMPLOYEES —

BOARD

VOLUNTEER LEADERSHIP COMMITTEES

STANDING COMMITTEES

CHIEF EXECUTIVE OFFICER
President or Executive VP
- Executive leadership
- Executive office spokesman

OFFICE OF PUBLIC RELATIONS
Director
- Liaison with public(s)
- Public/industry relations
- Public communications
- Press releases
- Press kits
- Schedule press conferences
- Information dissemination

OFFICE OF GOVERNMENT RELATIONS
Director
- Direction of the Office of Government Relations
- Government liaison
- Lobbying
- Provide Washington/state capitol "information watch"
- Address state chapters on Federal activities
- Testimony preparation

LINE ORGANIZATION CONTINUED ON NEXT PAGE

Organization for Management 51

THE TYPICAL LARGE ASSOCIATION
– OVER THIRTY EMPLOYEES –

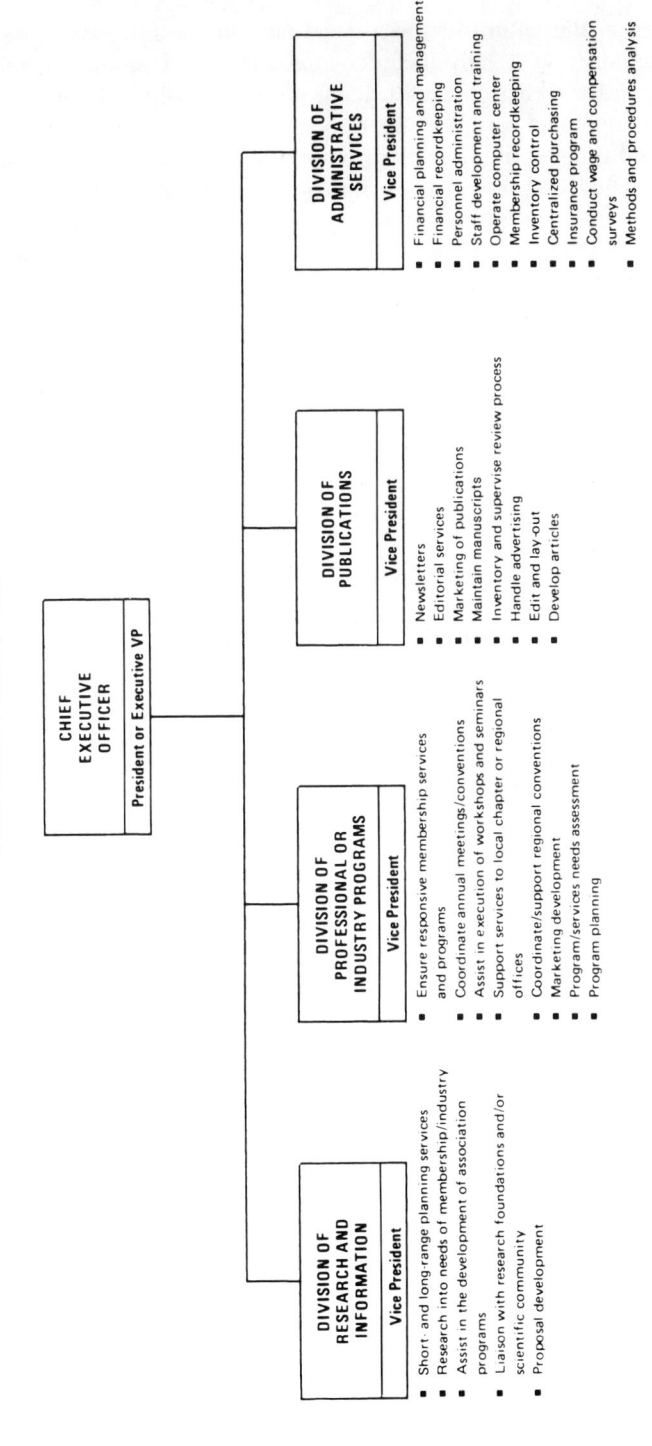

CHIEF EXECUTIVE OFFICER
President or Executive VP

DIVISION OF RESEARCH AND INFORMATION
Vice President

- Short- and long-range planning services
- Research into needs of membership/industry
- Assist in the development of association programs
- Liaison with research foundations and/or scientific community
- Proposal development

DIVISION OF PROFESSIONAL OR INDUSTRY PROGRAMS
Vice President

- Ensure responsive membership services and programs
- Coordinate annual meetings/conventions
- Assist in execution of workshops and seminars
- Support services to local chapter or regional offices
- Coordinate/support regional conventions
- Marketing development
- Program/services needs assessment
- Program planning

DIVISION OF PUBLICATIONS
Vice President

- Newsletters
- Editorial services
- Marketing of publications
- Maintain manuscripts
- Inventory and supervise review process
- Handle advertising
- Edit and lay-out
- Develop articles

DIVISION OF ADMINISTRATIVE SERVICES
Vice President

- Financial planning and management
- Financial recordkeeping
- Personnel administration
- Staff development and training
- Operate computer center
- Membership recordkeeping
- Inventory control
- Centralized purchasing
- Insurance program
- Conduct wage and compensation surveys
- Methods and procedures analysis

pending on the nature of the association and the interests of its members, the program also usually includes monitoring and promoting relevant legislation and tracking and influencing regulatory activity. The office of government relations is frequently responsible for preparing copy for a newsletter and other communications on legislative issues and activities. The director of government relations and other members of the office staff may be called upon to address state chapters or regional groups on federal or state governmental activities. They may help develop and operate mechanisms to provide accurate and timely information on legislative issues and activities and to organize volunteers to support legislation at the state level. In many cases, the large association's legislative program includes a political action committee which operates with a separate board of directors.

The "line" functions in the large association can be grouped logically into four major divisions:

- Research and Information,
- Professional or Industry Programs,
- Publications, and
- Administrative Services.

At this stage in the association's development it is not unusual to find each of the major divisions headed by a vice president. To draw a comparison with the organization structure for the developing association, the vice presidents function differently than the directors responsible for the divisions in the developing association. Although they have sound, adequate programmatic or technical knowledge, they are compensated more heavily for their managerial knowledge, skill, and ability. The technical expertise usually resides in the technical or specialty staff who make up the divisions. The role of the vice president is to function as an executive in the division: provide leadership and direction, develop plans and budgets, manage financial and staff resources, maintain contact with appropriate "publics" or constituencies, and serve on a management team with the chief staff executive to help guide the development of the association. The functions and scope of the major divisions in the large association are described in the remainder of this section.

The *division of research and information* consolidates these related functions under one senior executive who has overall responsibility for them. The division is concerned with developing short-range and long-range plans for the association, usually in cooperation with the chief staff executive and the board's planning committee. The role of the division staff in this activity is to conduct the necessary supporting research and accomplish the required staff work. This staff work includes the development of recommendations to help the chief staff executive and the board make effective decisions to guide the future development of the association.

The division staff also conducts research and generates ideas to support the development of relevant educational programs for the association membership or other constituencies if appropriate. In this capacity the division works closely with the division of professional and industry programs. To fulfill its responsibilities the division of research and information maintains contacts with research foundations, in some cases the association's own foundation, and with the scientific, professional, and industrial community that the association serves. Finally, the division may be responsible for developing proposals to obtain research contracts or grants for the industry, the members, or the association itself. In some cases, the division may include a department which obtains, executes, and manages grants and contracts.

The *division of professional or industry programs* has overall responsibility for ensuring that the membership is receiving responsive and relevant services. This responsibility usually includes the planning and coordination of annual meetings or conventions and assistance in the execution of workshops, seminars, and symposia. In addition, the division in most cases provides a variety of support services for local chapters and regional offices if they exist. These services include assistance in planning and conducting regional meetings and conventions.

Because of its link to the membership this division is usually responsible for membership development and the marketing of the association. This function may involve membership needs assessments to determine what services should be offered in order to retain members and attract new members. In conducting this research and in planning services, the division of professional or industry programs works closely with the division of research and information. In developing strategies to market the association and its programs, the division draws upon assistance from the office of public relations.

In a large association, the scope of responsibility of the *division of publications* varies significantly depending on the nature and size of the profession, industry, or other constituency served. The publications program may range from a single magazine or journal and an informal newsletter to a substantial publishing enterprise which includes books, manuals, journals, newsletters, and pamphlets. The smaller program, of course, requires fewer staff, usually with less expertise and experience. The staff frequently includes an editor who has technical knowledge of the profession or industry as well as editorial and publishing expertise, and supporting editorial staff. The complex publishing program may require a publications business manager and several editors, associate editors, assistant editors, and editorial assistants. In some cases, the majority of manuscripts for publications may be derived from members and other outside contributors.

In addition to the writing, editing, and publications support functions, the publications division in a large association (particularly when the publications program is extensive) is responsible for developing and executing advertising and marketing strategies to support the publications program. Therefore, the division staff may include an advertising manager or director and a supporting "sales" or promotion staff.

The *division of administrative services* in the large association resembles the business management and financial divisions of small corporations. The division frequently includes a financial department, a computer services department, a purchasing, sales, and inventory department (particularly if the association has a large publications program), a membership records department, a personnel department, and an office services department. The vice president of the division is a top-level financial and management executive with substantial training and experience.

The division is concerned with financial planning and management and develops supporting automated processing and information systems. In most cases, the association has its own computer, although it is possible that the systems are operated through a service bureau. If the association has a computer, the administrative services may include a data processing manager or director, programmers, systems analysts, and other data processing support personnel.

Once the association's staff has grown beyond 50 employees, it is not unusual to see the addition of a personnel officer who is responsible solely for personnel administration and its related functions. Depending on the actual size of the association, the position may be titled personnel director, manager, or coordinator. The personnel function is frequently concerned with more than routine recordkeeping and administrative activities. The personnel officer is responsible for staff development and training to ensure that employees continue to improve their knowledge, skills, and abilities in order to perform effectively in their current positions and to make them eligible for promotion to more responsible positions.

As noted at the outset of this chapter, there is a danger in trying to present typical associations since all associations are unique in some ways and cannot be described as typical for that reason. Nonetheless, a look at the evolution of association structures to determine how functions can be grouped at various stages of development may help association executives to develop solutions to organizational problems.

Chapter IV

DEFINING RESPONSIBILITIES: THE POSITION DESCRIPTION

This chapter emphasizes the need to define responsibilities clearly and accurately and it explores the means for doing so: the position description. The chapter describes uses for position descriptions, elements of position descriptions, and guidelines for preparing and maintaining position descriptions. At the end of the chapter, model position descriptions are presented for an array of positions commonly found in associations. However, they are not *complete* and should be used only as discussed in this chapter.

Uses for Position Descriptions

Earlier chapters stressed the importance of clarifying the roles of the volunteers and the professional staff and the need to organize association functions appropriately to support effective management. The next step is to ensure that responsibilities are clearly assigned and well defined. Good position descriptions are the most effective means of achieving this clarity. As an association grows and its functions become increasingly complex, it is not sufficient to assume that everyone understands his or her responsibilities or those of fellow staff members. It becomes critical to document responsibilities in writing.

In fact, position descriptions are an essential management tool. They are vital in many areas of the overall management process. They are needed to:

- Support the hiring and selection of personnel;
- Support effective performance appraisal;
- Identify and clarify lines of promotion within the association;

- Provide the basis for evaluating positions and establishing their relationship in the salary structure;
- Define qualification standards and assess training requirements;
- Help document the basis for hiring and firing decisions;
- Clarify lines of authority and prevent overlaps or gaps in responsibilities;
- Assess and modify the association's organizational structure;
- Clarify the work flow throughout the organization;
- Clarify appropriate channels of communication; and
- Support effective plans for staffing.

Position descriptions clearly can be used for a wide variety of purposes in managing the association's personnel. But they are not the solution for every situation and should be used carefully. Specifically:

- Position descriptions are not a quick fix for serious management or personnel problems. In fact, in developing thorough position descriptions where they have not existed before, an association may actually discover problems regarding responsibility assignments or a lack of clarity in the organizational structure.
- Position descriptions are not a superficial, paperwork exercise. To be effective the development and use of position descriptions must be part of the management process. The association's executives must be committed to making hard decisions where necessary to clarify responsibilities and establish lines of authority.
- Position descriptions are not merely descriptions of the incumbents in the jobs. Descriptions should be based on the positions and not the experience or abilities of the individuals who fill them.
- Position descriptions are not static. The association should not assume that it will be able to develop position descriptions once and never have to modify them. Organizations inevitably change, develop, grow. Positions usually change along with the organization itself. The descriptions must be updated and modified to reflect changes in the positions.

Elements of the Position Description

A good position description generally includes four categories of information or elements:

- Basic identification information such as title, assignment area (division or department), reporting relationships, other relationships;
- Summary of major functions: purpose, major elements, auxiliary responsibilities;
- Primary duties and responsibilities; and
- Qualifications: experience and educational requirements, necessary skill, special knowledge or ability.

These typical elements of a position description are presented as guidelines, but each association must select and define the elements that are appropriate to its needs as well as the format in which these elements will be documented.

For example, position descriptions that are to be compatible with the ASAE position classification system should contain the elements which are described below although they may appear in a different format. (Classified positions are those more easily identified with similar positions found in industry, government, or other associations. Salaries are usually based on market level for each occupational skill. Unclassified positions are not necessarily similar to positions found in other organizations. Salaries are based on job content analysis to evaluate components, complexity, responsibility, and authority.) There is no single right format for position descriptions, but the following may serve as a useful reference.

Classified Position

- **Position Title.** The formal title which will be used on employment records, correspondence, organization charts, etc.
- **Basic Function.** A succinct statement of the fundamental purpose of the position. This is a brief expansion of the position title.
- **Specific Responsibilities.** Concise, numbered statements of the individual functions the incumbent must perform to fully carry out the basic function. The responsibilities may be both technical and administrative; for example, supervising a staff of six persons (titles may be included), preparing an operating budget, etc.
- **Internal Relationships.** A statement of the personnel, by title, to whom the incumbent reports. Also, the identification of other association personnel (other than subordinates) with whom the incumbent will have contact in carrying out the job responsibilities.
- **External Relationships.** Identification of organizations and persons outside the association with whom the incumbent will have contact in carrying out the job responsibilities.
- **Qualifications.** Statement of the incumbent's mandatory and desired educational background, specific knowledge, skill and ability, prior experience, and any other requirements which uniquely describe the position.

Unclassified Position

- **Position Title.** The formal title which will be used on employment records, correspondence, organization charts, etc.
- **Basic Function.** A succinct statement of the fundamental purpose of the position. This is a brief expansion of the position title.
- **Specific Responsibilities.** Introduced by a statement of the scope of supervision, a numbered series of concise statements describing the

functions the incumbent must perform. The responsibilities should be both technical and managerial, such as the incumbent's role in policy formulation, planning, decision-making, supervision (numbers of persons, by title if appropriate), budget formulation and execution.
- **Internal Relations.** A statement of the personnel, by title, to whom the incumbent reports. Also, the identification of other association personnel other than subordinates with whom the incumbent will have contact in carrying out the job responsibilities.
- **External Relationships.** Identification of contacts the incumbent will have with members, the organization's governance structure, governmental bodies, other public and private organizations, and, if located elsewhere, the central office.
- **Qualifications.** Statement of the incumbent's mandatory and desired educational background, specific knowledge, skill and ability, experience, and any other requirements which uniquely describe the position.

Most of the elements are self-explanatory, but one element, specific responsibilities, warrants additional review. In fact, from an operational viewpoint, it can be said that the primary purpose of a position description is to describe the specific responsibilities the position involves. The other elements simply place the position in the organizational context to assist with administration.

In determining what specific responsibilities should be included in a position description, it is useful to ask a series of questions. Some of them deal with other elements of the position description but only for the purpose of determining entries in the specific responsibilities element. Here is a generic list of questions:
- What is the basic purpose of the position?
- What are the regular functions of the position—those performed on a daily basis?
- What are the other occasional functions?
- Do examples of occasional functions help to pinpoint the nature of the position?
- Who supervises the position?
- What positions does the position in question supervise?
- What degree of independent decision-making authority does the position carry?
- To what degree does the incumbent of the position plan or determine the activities of the position?
- What fiscal responsibility does the position have?
- What equipment does the incumbent of the position use in performing his or her responsibilities?
- What association records, if any, are maintained by the incumbent of the position?

- What internal and external contacts does the incumbent of the position have?

The amount of detail that is included in the position description to describe the responsibilities that are identified by answering these questions depends on the nature of the association and the types of positions that are involved. Some "experts" say position descriptions should be short and simple and avoid detail. Others believe that detail is essential to ensure that the position description accurately presents the responsibilities of the position and leaves little room for ambiguity or confusion. One of the problems in very detailed position descriptions is that they may be so restrictive that there is not sufficient flexibility to add an occasional "extra" assignment. An employee may legitimately say: "That's not part of my job." But the simple and concise description should not be construed as incomplete or inaccurate. It can clearly reflect the scope of the position and cover all major aspects of the assigned responsibilities.

Regardless of the relative merits of these theories, the essential purpose of the position description is to describe and analyze all job requirements as clearly and concisely as possible. Rarely would it be necessary to document every single task a person in the position might perform. However, if there are fairly frequent variations in the position, they should be noted. If occasional or incidental assignments are significant to the effective performance of the position, the variety, limits, and time requirements of those assignments should be addressed in the description.

The fundamental rule is to ensure that the position responsibilities are clear and understandable—even to someone who is not knowledgeable of the job. There are some steps which can be followed to help ensure this clarity:

- All related duties should be presented together in the position description. It is difficult to understand the scope of a position if similar responsibilities are scattered throughout the position description.
  - List duties and responsibilities on the basis of their importance to the effective execution of the position—beginning with most important, then second most important, etc.
  - List duties according to the frequency with which they are performed—beginning with the function carried out most often.
  - List duties and responsibilities in sequential order if there is a pattern in the position function.
- Clearly specify the scope and limits of responsibilities. Appropriately descriptive words should be selected to ensure that there is no doubt about the actual responsibilities.
- Spell out differences in responsibilities. Certain types of positions are similar regardless of the departments in which they are located—for example, a clerk typist position. But the position description should

identify things which may differentiate one clerk typist job from another.

Preparing the Position Description

Who Should Prepare the Position Descriptions?

There is no single right answer to the question of who should prepare position descriptions. It depends upon a number of factors: the size of the association, the number of descriptions being developed at any given time, the nature, experience, and abilities of the association's staff, and other conditions which may be relevant to the process.

Some associations bring in outside consultants to develop position descriptions because they do not have staff with the appropriate experience or skill; they want to ensure objectivity; or their staff do not have time to undertake the task. Some large associations have a personnel officer or perhaps even a position analyst whose responsibilities include the development and maintenance of up-to-date position descriptions for all association positions. A small association may identify an employee with the requisite skills and assign the development of position descriptions as a special project. Other associations may simply have the incumbents and the supervisors work together in developing position descriptions which are then reviewed by higher level supervisors.

If the association does not already have position descriptions or is undertaking a major revision of the descriptions, and does not have a personnel officer or analyst, it is probably wise to bring in outside assistance or to designate a staff member to undertake the project as a special assignment. This approach is likely to ensure greater objectivity and consistency in the development of the descriptions.

Writing Style

If the writing style used in position descriptions is confusing, it may contribute to or cause problems in various aspects of personnel administration: hiring and promotion, performance appraisal, and salary administration. Language used in position descriptions should be clear and concise. But the descriptions should also contain all the information necessary to adequately define the scope of the job responsibilities.

Here are some general guidelines for the writing style:
- Use the present tense.
- Begin sentences with active verbs.
- Tell what, not how. The details of how a responsibility is carried out belong in separate operating instructions.
- Be precise in defining duties. Where occasional duties are performed, examples should be given to ensure that the nature of those duties is clearly understood.

- Avoid using "may" whenever possible.
- Avoid the use of verbs which are not precise in definition—such as "handles" and "deals with."
- Use simple, straightforward language, avoid ambiguous words and phrases, and avoid extraneous words, especially adjectives.
- Define the scope of authority and degree of supervision. The word "supervise" should not be used if only occasional contact occurs rather than ongoing supervision. Also, the position description should distinguish between "technical" supervision and "administrative" supervision.
- Avoid specialized jargon or unnecessary technical language. Since position descriptions are used by numerous people in the association, they must be written in language that anyone can understand regardless of the knowledge of the position.

In some instances the writing style may be influenced by the type of position that is being described. For example, clerical positions usually consist of relatively specific tasks which can be described easily in a "narrative-type" style. Staff positions, on the other hand, include responsibilities which are less precise or concrete. Therefore, descriptions for those positions often focus on the responsibilities of particular positions rather than on specific tasks.

Gathering Information For Position Descriptions

Writing good position descriptions is dependent upon the collection of complete and accurate information. Effective information collection requires cooperation from the incumbents of positions. Generally, there are four methods which are used to obtain position information.
1. Direct observation of an incumbent performing on the job.
2. Interviews with incumbents and their supervisors.
3. Position questionnaires.
4. Job logs and other records.

In selecting an appropriate method, the association should consider the various advantages and disadvantages of each.
- Direct observation of the performance gives the person developing the description first-hand information about the specific functions and the skill and knowledge required. It offers the advantage of being totally objective if handled appropriately. The "observer" must watch the employee perform all the basic functions of the position as well as any incidental responsibilities which are critical to its evaluation.
This method is time consuming. Also, it is most appropriate for evaluating positions for which the functions are relatively clear-cut. It

is more difficult to observe, in a reasonable period of time, all aspects of a position that has a variety of complex responsibilities, involves knowledge of policies, and requires important decision making. Finally, the accuracy and value of this method can be affected greatly by the skill of the "observer" and by the employee's reaction to being observed.
- Interviews with incumbents and their supervisors can be valuable in providing comprehensive and in-depth information about functions and responsibilities. The interviewer can probe aspects of the position which might not be clear through direct observation.

  But there are also possible disadvantages to this method of obtaining position information. The interviewer must be skilled in the process and have a basic understanding of the position functions. If he or she is not, the interview can get off focus and fail to provide a comprehensive view of the position. Many incumbents tend to move easily to a discussion of problems or complaints when asked to talk about their responsibilities. The interviewer must be able to keep the interview on track. Also, some employees may have difficulty articulating their functions and responsibilities accurately.
- Questionnaires are usually most helpful as a supplement to the direct observation or interview methods already described. In preparing a questionnaire it is difficult to ensure that all aspects of every position will be covered. Also, written answers can sometimes be confusing to the person who must use them in developing position descriptions.
- Job logs also provide a means for supplementing information obtained through one of the other methods. The incumbent of the position maintains a written sequential record of functions performed over a period of time sufficient to ensure that the basic aspects of the position will be covered. The record also notes the amount of time required for the tasks listed. Job logs alone are rarely used to develop position descriptions since they are likely to be narrow in scope, failing to cover important points such as skill required, equipment used, and job conditions. A job log may also fail to reveal important seasonal functions.

The association's staff must determine the most appropriate method to use in obtaining job information. The observation and job log methods are relatively clear cut, but the interviews and questionnaires are more complicated. Here are some basic guidelines to follow to help ensure that they are effective.

Interviews
- Since the interview process is such an important step in developing good job descriptions, the person conducting the interviews—the "an-

alyst"—should be an experienced interviewer and should be able to put the incumbent at ease.
- The inteviewer should be familiar with the positions for which descriptions are being developed and have a good understanding of the association's organization and how the positions fit in with the association's purpose and functions.
- The interviewer should have a prepared questionnaire for use in conducting the interviews.
- Both the employee and the supervisor should be advised in advance that a position description is being developed and that an interview must be conducted for that purpose. This step will ensure that both the supervisor and the employee are comfortable with the process and understand why it is being done. Also, they will be able to arrange the interview at a time which is convenient and does not greatly interfere with the employee's work.
- To ensure that there is adequate time for a complete interview, two hours should be set aside. The interview should be conducted in a setting where privacy and freedom from interruptions can be assured.
- At the outset of the interview, the analyst should explain the purpose of the interview and how the results will be used in developing the position description. A special effort should be made to reassure the incumbent that the purpose of the interview and the related process is to obtain a clear and precise understanding of the position in question—not to evaluate the person's qualifications or performance in the position.
- If the position under consideration involves responsibility for supervising numerous other positions, the interviewer should gain an understanding of the basic responsibilities of each of those positions and the degree to which the supervisor is involved in execution of the duties.
- The interviewer should listen carefully to clearly understand the incumbent's responsibilities and take accurate notes. The interviewer should allow the incumbent to choose his or her own words in describing the position and not take issue with the incumbent's statements.
- The analyst should discourage discussion of grievances or complaints about supervisors or colleagues.
- The interviewer should avoid any discussion of salary and make it clear to the employee that salaries are not under consideration in the position description process.
- In conducting the interview and in preparing the position description, the analyst should guard against being influenced by personal likes or dislikes.

Questionnaires

One benefit of using a questionnaire to collect job information is that it helps the analyst and the incumbent organize the content of the position. The questionnaire itself must be clear, complete, and well organized. It should solicit information about the following:

- **Position Identification.** Title, short summary of basic function, reporting relationship, salary level, average working hours including any overtime which may be required.
- **Position Requirements.** Education, experience, technical or other special knowledge, supervisory skill, use of equipment.
- **Position Responsibilities.** Supervisory responsibilities—both individual and group leadership, budget responsibilities, internal and external contacts, policy responsibilities, equipment responsibility.
- **Effort Demanded.** Decision making, planning, level of concentration, accuracy, time requirements, pressure level.

Reviewing the Position Information

When all the information has been collected, the analyst should carefully review the information for each position to ensure that it appears accurate and is complete. The analyst should be alert to instances where employees may have exaggerated their responsibilities or where they may have failed to provide a complete picture of the scope and responsibilities of their positions. If there are problems, it may be necessary to conduct follow-up interviews with some employees.

After reviewing the information, the analyst should draft descriptions for each position. At this point in the position description process, the analyst will require the full cooperation of the respective supervisors, the personnel department, and the appropriate division or department heads. They must review the draft descriptions to determine if the information is complete. Does the description represent the positions accurately? Have responsibilities been distorted in any way? Does the description reflect the most effective organization of tasks? It is particularly critical that the supervisor of a position review the description carefully at this stage to verify that the scope of responsibilities and duties are accurate as outlined.

Once the supervisors and other reviewers have submitted their comments on the descriptions, the analyst should revise them as necessary. It is important to ensure consistency and conformity in all the position descriptions throughout the association—in terms of titles, responsibility descriptions, and so forth. The analyst should also be sure to identify the critical factors which distinguish any position from others in the organization.

Final Approval of Position Descriptions

When all the reviews are complete and all information has been verified, the analyst should present the final draft to the incumbent for discussion with the supervisor, department head, or other appropriate official. This final review is the incumbent's last opportunity to note any disagreement or recommend changes. After the employee's final comments, the immediate supervisor, department or division heads, and the personnel office, if appropriate, should "sign-off" on the description, making it official.

Maintaining Position Descriptions

Once position descriptions are developed, it is critical that they be maintained. As positions change, the descriptions must be revised and updated accordingly. In some associations position descriptions are maintained on an irregular or informal basis without any problems. In others this approach is ineffective, and descriptions easily and frequently become obsolete. Therefore, it is usually best if the association establishes regular procedures for keeping them up to date. Many approaches are in use.

- Some associations use the annual performance appraisal as an opportunity to review position duties and responsibilities. The supervisor and the incumbent discuss whether there have been significant changes which may require revision of the position description. Recommendations for changes are then made to the personnel officer or an appropriate supervisor.
- Some associations require that the position analyst or personnel officer (or person serving in a similar capacity) review the position descriptions with the incumbents periodically to assess whether there have been substantive changes.
- Some associations request department heads and employees to call for a review of the position, and consequently the description, when they believe the position has changed.

The development of accurate, useful position descriptions requires that the association commit a significant amount of time and expense. And the results can often have unforeseen consequences. The process often identifies and brings to the surface smoldering conflicts or disputes about responsibility and authority and sensitive "turf" issues. However, these problems should be addressed and resolved in any case. In the end, the overall benefits of the process and the usefulness of the completed position descriptions make the effort worthwhile.

Model Position Descriptions

This last section of the chapter contains model descriptions for positions most commonly found in the headquarters staff of associations. Each association is unique. It must be organized and staffed to accomplish its specific mission. A position in one association is never totally interchangeable with one in another association. Yet there is often a great deal of similarity, at least in the basic functions, between like positions in associations. Accordingly, the model position descriptions in this section state only the most *common* features. They do *not* constitute *complete* position descriptions. You will have to decide the content of the position descriptions of your association, of which the elements in the model position descriptions are only a part, as well as the format you will use.

Use of the Model Position Descriptions

Here are seven basic steps for an association to follow in selecting a model position description and using it to prepare staff job descriptions:

1. Review the content and format the association has adopted for position descriptions, using as a guide the section titled Elements of the Position Description.
2. Review the model position descriptions. Look at both the position title and the basic functions. The best model is the one with a statement of basic functions which most closely matches the needs of the association.
3. Tailor the statement of basic functions to the association, and change the position title if necessary.
4. Analyze the specific responsibilities and change, add, or delete until the list adequately describes what a person in the job should do. (Remember—information on *how* the work is done should be documented separately.)
5. Write the internal and external relationships sections.
6. Complete the other sections required by the standard contents determined in Step 1 above.
7. Integrate the position description into the association's personnel or position classification system, adding any other necessary data elements, and take whatever next steps the personnel system requires, i.e., concurrences, classification, approval, budget coordination, etc.

In using the model position descriptions, remember that:
- There is nothing magic in the titles. Use the association's own.
- The functions and responsibilities are simply typical, and each association must decide what is appropriate for its needs.
- The reporting relationships are also only examples, and the association must decide the appropriate relationships based on careful organizational analysis.

POSITION DESCRIPTIONS FOR ASSOCIATION STAFF

IMPORTANT

Use the model position descriptions in this section only as a part of the process presented in Chapter IV.

Position descriptions included in this section reflect functional responsibilities normally identified with the indicated occupational titles. Actual responsibilities assigned in any given association will vary depending on the mission, size and organizational structure of each association. Hence, the position descriptions that follow should be used only as guides and points of departure.

The format used by an association for preparing actual position descriptions should be tailored to meet its own administrative needs. Some of the elements that should be formally included (even though they are not included in the position descriptions that follow) are:

- Organizational unit, i.e. department, division etc.
- Title of supervisor to whom person reports
- Relevant prior experience required
- Educational requirements
- Technical skills necessary
- Budgetary responsibilities
- Authority to make final decisions without approval of supervisors
- Supervisory responsibilities
- Supervision received
- Planning responsibilities
- Role in policy formulation

Each association will attribute more or less importance to the several elements listed above and must decide for itself which elements to incorporate in its position description format. Also, each association must decide for itself how these elements will be used in (1) classifying positions for salary purposes; (2) assessing the qualifications of candidates to fill positions; and (3) evaluating employee performance.

Accordingly, the model position descriptions should be viewed simply as a starting point for an association wishing to establish a formalized system of position descriptions.

POSITION TITLE: Chief Staff Executive

BASIC FUNCTION:

Serves as the chief executive officer, responsible to the board of directors for the effective conduct of the affairs of the association. Recommends and participates in board formulation of association mission, goals, and objectives and related policies. Within that framework plans, organizes, coordinates, controls, and directs the staff, programs, and activities of the association.

SPECIFIC RESPONSIBILITIES:

Within the limits of the charter and by-laws of the association and policies established by the board of directors, the chief staff executive, with appropriate delegations:

1. Establishes the organization structure for the headquarters office and the related staffing structure.
2. Establishes administrative policies and procedures for headquarters functions.
3. Recruits, hires, and trains staff and administers an effective personnel program which includes position descriptions, performance standards, performance appraisals, and a compensation system.
4. Develops and supervises an effective program of membership development and membership services.
5. Develops and maintains a publications program which is responsive to the needs of the membership.
6. Develops and conducts an education program to advance the professional/technical/managerial skills of the membership.
7. Organizes and conducts an annual conference which includes programs, exhibits, and other events consistent with the objectives of the association.
8. Conducts research necessary to the association and informs the board, elected officials, and membership as appropriate.
9. Maintains effective internal and external public relations.
10. Serves as spokesman for the association in conjunction with the chief elected officer.
11. Maintains an effective government affairs program to represent the interests of the association membership to Congress and government agencies as appropriate.
12. Manages the finances of the association, including the preparation of an annual budget and long-range forecasts of needs.
13. Ensures the legal integrity of the association.
14. Plans and coordinates meetings of the board of directors and the elected officials of the association.
15. Provides periodic reports to the board of directors along with recommendations.
16. Monitors and assists committees of the board and the elected officials.

INTERNAL RELATIONSHIPS:

Key staff executives and directors report to the chief staff executive. Has occasional contact with other association staff.

EXTERNAL RELATIONSHIPS:

Has regular contact with the elected officials and the board of directors and its committees on policy matters and other issues as appropriate. Maintains personal contact with regional, state, or chapter organizations and the general membership to the greatest degree possible. Maintains appropriate relationships with other associations, industry, government, public service organizations, and vendors to enhance the image of the association and the attainment of its objectives.

POSITION TITLE: Deputy Chief Staff Executive

BASIC FUNCTION:

Assists the chief staff executive by carrying out those chief executive officer responsibilities which are delegated and by assuming all of the chief staff executive's responsibilities in his or her absence.

SPECIFIC RESPONSIBILITIES:

In addition to the general sharing, as stated under Basic Function, of the responsibilities of the chief staff executive, the deputy chief staff executive is responsible on a permanent basis for staffing selected member committees and handles special projects or activities that require attention at the executive level. The deputy chief staff executive usually plays a major role in preparing issues for board meetings and in developing the association's budget. In most associations the deputy chief staff executive is also assigned ongoing responsibility for selected association activities. These responsibilities vary depending on the nature and site of the association and other related factors.

INTERNAL RELATIONSHIPS:

Reports to the chief staff executive and has regular contact with the management staff of the headquarters. Receives support from the administrative assistant who reports to the chief staff executive.

EXTERNAL RELATIONSHIPS:

Has regular contact with the elected officers and the board of directors and its committees, subject to approval by chief staff executive. Maintains personal contact with the membership to the greatest degree possible. Maintains appropriate relations with other associations, industry, government, public service organizations, and vendors to enhance the image of the association and the attainment of its objectives. Communicates external contacts to the chief staff executive to ensure adequate coordination.

POSITION TITLE: Director of Administrative Services

BASIC FUNCTION:

Supervises the administrative and business management functions of the association headquarters consistent with policy direction of the chief staff executive, and the goals and objectives of the association. The director of administrative services provides, through the various departments of the division, professional assistance and support to all organizational elements of the headquarters in the conduct of the business and administrative aspects of their functional activities.

SPECIFIC RESPONSIBILITIES:

1. Manages the division and provides direction, coordination, and motivation of divisional and departmental personnel.
2. Administers an orderly personnel program which integrates recruiting, hiring, training, position descriptions, performance standards, performance appraisals, and compensation (including group insurance and pension programs).
3. Supervises the financial management program of the association. Assures the development of annual and long-range budgets which are based on analysis of trends in membership, subscriptions, sales, general economic trends, and the status of the profession/industry. Ensures adequate handling of and accounting for the association's funds.
4. Establishes and maintains a membership records system which provides basic data on the status of each member and additional data useful for research in support of association plans and programs.
5. Provides a data processing capability to support the association's financial program, membership records, and other appropriate activities.
6. Supervises the association's purchasing and contacting activities, ensuring the most economical use of association funds for supplies and services.
7. Provides other administrative services such as mail and distribution.
8. Monitors the performance of assigned departments on recurring and special activities and, as appropriate, informs the chief staff executive.
9. Monitors the physical plant.
10. Performs other administrative duties as requested by the chief staff executive.

INTERNAL RELATIONSHIPS:

Reports to the chief staff executive or the deputy chief staff executive. Has regular contacts with all management personnel within the association.

EXTERNAL RELATIONSHIPS:

Has regular contact with vendors of supplies and services. Frequent contact with field offices concerning administrative matters.

POSITION TITLE: Advertising Manager

BASIC FUNCTION:

Secures advertising for association publications.

SPECIFIC RESPONSIBILITIES:

1. Maintains knowledge of the objectives and activities of the association to identify likely advertisers.
2. Contacts current and potential advertisers to solicit advertising in association publications.
3. Plans and implements promotional programs to increase advertising volume.
4. Determines effective prospect gathering methods, maintains effective prospect mailing lists, and makes periodic contacts with prospects.
5. Plans and promotes, in coordination with the director of publications, special publications which promote the association and attract advertising.
6. Coordinates advertising schedules, promotions, and editorial content with the publications editor.
7. Coordinates the design, layout, and mark-up of advertising when required.
8. Plans and coordinates association publication exhibits at conferences and meetings.
9. Compiles information from similar or competitive publications (rate cards, market demographics, circulation reports, etc.) to determine their strengths and weaknesses and to generate sound ideas.

INTERNAL RELATIONSHIPS:

Reports to the director of publications. Has regular contact with the publications editor and frequent contact with program staff.

EXTERNAL RELATIONSHIPS:

Has extensive contacts with current and potential advertisers and with other advertising sales personnel.

POSITION TITLE: Chief Staff Attorney

BASIC FUNCTION:

Ensures the legal integrity of the association and its central office operations.

SPECIFIC RESPONSIBILITIES:
1. Maintains the organizing documents of the association and makes required reports.
2. Identifies and monitors federal, state, and/or local legislation which impacts the industry; assists in preparing legislative proposals.
3. Provides legal advice concerning association activities and initiatives.
4. Reviews central and field office employment policies and provides legal counsel concerning employment issues.
5. Provides legal review of contracts and leases for central office and field offices.
6. Reviews the association budget and financial procedures for tax or other legal implications.

INTERNAL RELATIONSHIPS:

Reports to the chief staff executive or the deputy chief staff executive. Has regular contact with executives and managers in association central staff.

EXTERNAL RELATIONSHIPS:

Has frequent contact with the elected officials, the board of directors and its committees, field offices, members, and government legislative bodies and executive agencies.

POSITION TITLE: Chapter Relations Director

BASIC FUNCTION:

Promotes good relations between the association headquarters and individual chapters and districts.

SPECIFIC RESPONSIBILITIES:

1. Acts as the focal point and clearinghouse for headquarters transactions with the chapters.
2. Develops and executes a chapter relations program.
3. Ensures that all chapters are contacted on a regular basis, maintaining continuous two-way communication.
4. Answers all queries from chapters regarding association operations, in coordination with appropriate association executives and managers.
5. Maintains a chapter operating manual and assists the chapters in using it.
6. Assists district chairmen in developing new chapters.
7. Maintains contact with district chairmen and promotes an interchange of information.
8. Maintains a district chairman's manual and assists in its implementation.
9. Serves as headquarters focal point for organizing and conducting district conferences.

INTERNAL RELATIONSHIPS:

Reports to the chief staff executive or the deputy chief staff executive. Works closely with all of the association's executives and managers.

EXTERNAL RELATIONSHIPS:

Has regular contact with district and chapter officials and with association members.

POSITION TITLE: Director of Consumer Affairs

BASIC FUNCTION:

Serves as focal point for the association headquarters and the membership regarding relations between the industry and consumers of its products/services.

SPECIFIC RESPONSIBILITIES:
1. Solicits information from members regarding their consumer relations policies and programs.
2. Monitors the press and other media for information regarding consumer attitudes toward the industry.
3. Monitors legislative and regulatory actions regarding changes which affect consumers.
4. Visits members to become familiar with their products/services and views toward consumers.
5. Collaborates with the chief economist, the technical director, and others, in drafting articles for publication, within the association and in public media, about the interests and actions of the industry/profession regarding consumer views.
6. Drafts proposed association response to direct contacts by consumers.

INTERNAL RELATIONSHIPS:

Reports to the chief staff executive, deputy chief staff executive, or program director. Works with the chief economist, public relations director, director of government relations, and other executives and managers on staff.

EXTERNAL RELATIONSHIPS:

Has frequent communication with members and with the general public.

POSITION TITLE: Controller

BASIC FUNCTION:

Administers the financial affairs of the association and recommends cost-effective management systems.

SPECIFIC RESPONSIBILITIES:

1. Maintains detailed awareness of the financial affairs of the association and takes or recommends appropriate actions.
2. Establishes the chart of accounts.
3. Ensures the adequacy of accounting practices, handling of funds, internal controls, and reporting to government agencies.
4. Ensures timely and accurate reporting of financial information and makes recommendations.
5. Evaluates association work processes and programs for cost-effectiveness.
6. Handles association investments.
7. Coordinates preparation of the annual budget under direction of the chief staff executive or deputy chief staff executive.
8. Advises the chief staff executive and other executives and managers regarding financial management.
9. Arranges annual independent audits of the association's financial operations.

INTERNAL RELATIONSHIPS:

Reports to the chief staff executive, deputy chief staff executive, or director of administrative services. Works closely with all of the association's executives and managers.

EXTERNAL RELATIONSHIPS:

Has contact with the treasurer, auditors, banks, attorneys, and executives of other associations or related organizations.

POSITION TITLE: Convention and Meetings Director

BASIC FUNCTION:

Plans, organizes, and coordinates the association's annual convention and major meetings.

SPECIFIC RESPONSIBILITIES:
1. Proposes and develops the convention theme.
2. Develops the detailed convention program in conjunction with the appropriate association volunteers and staff executives.
3. Arranges participation of speakers and related logistics.
4. Inspects prospective convention sites and makes appropriate recommendations.
5. Makes all arrangements with hotel/site managers.
6. Hires and supervises the activities of service contractors supporting the convention.
7. Arranges for all supplies and materials needed for conventions/meetings.
8. Develops convention program book, exhibitors directory, and registration kits.
9. Promotes convention exhibits and coordinates their placement and operation.
10. Supervises convention registration and floor management.
11. Conducts post-convention evaluation and prepares report.

INTERNAL RELATIONSHIPS:

Reports to the chief staff executive or the deputy chief staff executive. Has regular contact with the association's executives and managers involved in conventions and meetings.

EXTERNAL RELATIONSHIPS:

Has extensive contact with hotel and site managers, exhibitors, and service contractors. Has frequent contact with convention directors of other associations.

POSITION TITLE: Data Processing Manager

BASIC FUNCTION:

Provides automated data processing services for all association functions.

SPECIFIC RESPONSIBILITIES:

1. Analyzes association business and program operations to identify data transactions and determine the feasibility of computer support.
2. Recommends appropriate computer input, storage and retrieval, processing and output equipment, and related communications devices for the optimum response to the association's needs.
3. Obtains or prepares computer software programs for authorized computer applications.
4. Monitors data inputs for timeliness and accuracy.
5. Operates and maintains the computer and related hardware.
6. Reviews computer outputs for timeliness and accuracy, and assists users in understanding them.
7. Generates special reports.

INTERNAL RELATIONSHIPS:

Reports to the director of administration. Has frequent contact with the association's executives and managers who use, or are potential users of, automated data processing.

EXTERNAL RELATIONSHIPS:

Works with equipment suppliers. Has frequent contact with data processing managers of other organizations.

POSITION TITLE: Chief Economist

BASIC FUNCTION:

Evaluates current status of the association and plans for the future in the context of the total economic environment.

SPECIFIC RESPONSIBILITIES:
1. Maintains knowledge of the economy and the status and trends of expenditures related to the association.
2. Obtains economic data and conducts research, on own initiative or on request, related to the industry or profession.
3. Develops, for the association journal and newsletter, articles presenting factual material concerning the industry or profession and policy issues which must be faced.
4. Answers inquiries from association executives, managers, and members.
5. Participates in policy planning and budgeting activities.

INTERNAL RELATIONSHIPS:

Reports to the chief staff executive, deputy chief staff executive, or director of information and research. Has frequent contact with program staff.

EXTERNAL RELATIONSHIPS:

Communicates regularly with government offices and research organizations.

POSITION TITLE: Director of Education

BASIC FUNCTION:

Plans and administers the educational activities conducted by the association headquarters and counsels and assists in educational activities of districts and chapters.

SPECIFIC RESPONSIBILITIES:

1. Designs and administers a continuous process for determining those education and training needs of the membership which can be met through the efforts of the association headquarters.
2. Analyzes education and training needs of the membership and identifies workshops, seminars, symposia, convention events, and other offerings which meet those needs.
3. Coordinates the development of educational and training textbooks, workbooks, articles, and audiovisual materials.
4. Designs a continuing education program which makes available to the membership the association's educational offerings.
5. Maintains records of participation in the continuing education program.
6. Assists districts and chapters in the design and conduct of local educational and training activities.
7. Serves as instructor in selected educational offerings.
8. Plans and coordinates the educational segment of the annual convention and meetings.
9. Assists in the design and conduct of a staff development program for employees of the association headquarters.

INTERNAL RELATIONSHIPS:

Reports to the chief staff executive or the deputy chief staff executive. Has frequent contact with program officials, the membership director, and the director of publications.

EXTERNAL RELATIONSHIPS:

Communicates frequently with experts in educational program subject areas, educational institutions and firms, districts, chapters, and individual members.

POSITION TITLE: Employer-Employee Relations Director

BASIC FUNCTION:

Serves as primary advisor to association executives and member organizations on matters relating to labor relations.

SPECIFIC RESPONSIBILITIES:

1. Collects and maintains information on the status of labor relations of member organizations.
2. Monitors federal, state, and local legislation and regulations involving labor relations.
3. Provides an exchange of information on labor relations matters between member organizations, directly and in the association newsletter.
4. Conducts research on labor on own initiative and in response to inquiries.
5. Organizes and conducts workshops on labor relations for labor relations personnel of member organizations.
6. Counsels member organizations regarding specific labor relations issues and assists in on-site arbitration.

INTERNAL RELATIONSHIPS:

Reports to the chief staff executive or the deputy chief staff executive.

EXTERNAL RELATIONSHIPS:

Has contact with executives and labor relations staff of member organizations, with union officials, with governmental agencies, and with labor relations officials of other associations.

POSITION TITLE: Field Staff Director

BASIC FUNCTION:

Serves as focal point for association headquarters with field staff.

SPECIFIC RESPONSIBILITIES:
1. Receives communications from regional offices, and collaborates with appropriate association executives and managers to prepare headquarters responses.
2. Receives and disseminates regional office reports on statistics and activities, and advises appropriate headquarters staff.
3. Analyzes regional office activity and makes recommendations.
4. Maintains the regional office operations manual and assists the regional offices in implementation.

INTERNAL RELATIONSHIPS:

Reports to the chief staff executive or deputy chief staff executive. Works closely with the membership and information and research offices.

EXTERNAL RELATIONSHIPS:

Has regular contact with regional offices and frequent contact with members.

POSITION TITLE: Director of Government Relations

BASIC FUNCTION:

Monitors federal and state legislative and regulatory activities which relate to the association and recommends and coordinates the association's response.

SPECIFIC RESPONSIBILITIES:
1. Establishes personal contact with members of Congress and their staff and with key policy and program officials in federal and state departments and agencies.
2. Monitors legislative, regulatory, and program activities which affect the association and informs the chief staff executive.
3. Coordinates the development of association responses to legislative and regulatory actions.
4. Provides testimony to Congress and submits proposed legislation and comments.
5. Analyzes legislative and regulatory trends, and the political philosophy of key legislators and administration officials.
6. Keeps the staff executives informed regarding legislative and regulatory activity and informs the membership through newsletters and special communications.
7. Files lobbying and federal election campaign reports required by the government.
8. Counsels districts and chapters regarding local government relations.

INTERNAL RELATIONSHIPS:

Reports to the chief staff executive or the deputy chief staff executive. Communicates frequently with the elected association officers and executives in the association's headquarters.

EXTERNAL RELATIONSHIPS:

Has frequent personal contact with senators, representatives, and their staff and with department and agency officials. Regular contacts with government relations officers of other associations.

POSITION TITLE: Director of Government Relations (Washington Office)

BASIC FUNCTION:

Coordinates the association's federal government liaison and lobbying activities. Assists state association government liaison activities and provides copy for association publications.

SPECIFIC RESPONSIBILITIES:

1. Maintains liaison with departments and agencies of the federal government that are responsible for policies and programs that relate to the association, and with members of Congress and the administration.
2. Monitors legislative and regulatory actions and informs the chief staff executive.
3. Develops, in coordination with the chief staff executive, appropriate association responses to legislation and regulations.
4. Provides, in coordination with the chief staff executive, association responses to requests for information or comment by government agencies.
5. Coordinates, as approved by the chief staff executive, activities with other associations regarding legislative or regulatory matters of common interest.
6. Prepares copy regarding government activities for association publications.
7. Supervises Washington office staff.

INTERNAL RELATIONSHIPS:

Reports to the chief staff executive or the deputy chief staff executive. Has regular contact with all management personnel in the association headquarters, particularly in program areas.

EXTERNAL RELATIONSHIPS:

Has extensive contact with members of Congress and the administration, representatives of other associations, and state and chapter representatives of the association.

POSITION TITLE: Director of Information and Research

BASIC FUNCTION:

Collects, organizes, and disseminates information on the industry or profession of the members.

SPECIFIC RESPONSIBILITIES:
1. Gathers and maintains information on member characteristics and practices, as well as general information, which is appropriate for use by the headquarters staff and the membership.
2. Conducts research on topics of interest to members
3. Collects information on trends and developments in industry or profession.
4. Develops, or arranges for the development of, timely materials to inform the members regarding selected topics.
5. Conducts research and statistical surveys and commissions manuscripts and textbooks.

INTERNAL RELATIONSHIPS:

Reports to the chief staff executive or deputy chief staff executive. Has frequent contact with central staff executives and managers.

EXTERNAL RELATIONS:

Has frequent contact with members, field offices, and information and research officials of other public and private organizations.

POSITION TITLE: Director of Marketing

BASIC FUNCTION:

Maintains, interprets, and disseminates industry-wide marketing information and acts as industry marketing spokesman to associations and companies in other industries.

SPECIFIC RESPONSIBILITIES:
1. Maintains market information and statistics regarding the industry.
2. Conducts marketing studies on own initiative and on request.
3. Identifies trends in industry-wide marketing and prepares forecasts.
4. Provides industry liaison with major companies in consumer industries and with government agencies.
5. Prepares articles and news releases for association publications.

INTERNAL RELATIONSHIPS:

Reports to the chief staff executive or the deputy chief staff executive. Has frequent contact with the chief economist and director of information and research.

EXTERNAL RELATIONSHIPS:

Communicates regularly with members, regional offices, national committees, associations, major companies of client industries, and government agencies.

POSITION TITLE: Membership Director

BASIC FUNCTION:

Develops and maintains membership in the association and directs service programs for members.

SPECIFIC RESPONSIBILITIES:
1. Develops and administers a process for identifying, recruiting, and registering potential members.
2. Ensures maintenance of membership records in sufficient detail to support communications and research.
3. Ensures that membership directory is compiled in cooperation with publications department.
4. Publishes periodic reports on membership status and membership development.
5. Analyzes the membership and recommends steps for retention and expansion.
6. Serves as point of contact for individual members seeking information or assistance on membership.
7. Supplies information for member billings and subscriptions; monitors member dues status and fulfillment of subscriptions and other services to members.

INTERNAL RELATIONSHIPS:

Reports to the chief staff executive, deputy chief staff executive, or director of administrative services. Has frequent contact with the accounting department and the director of publications.

EXTERNAL RELATIONSHIPS:

Communicates with members either individually in response to queries or collectively through the journal and newsletter. Communicates with other managers to prepare responses to member queries.

POSITION TITLE: Personnel Manager

BASIC FUNCTION:

Administers the personnel program for the association's headquarters staff.

SPECIFIC RESPONSIBILITIES:

1. Administers the association's employee recruiting, selection, and training program.
2. Ensures compliance with equal opportunity legislation and the association's affirmative action program.
3. Prepares and files government reports such as workmen's compensation claims, manpower reports, EEO-1, and ERISA returns.
4. Manages the daily activities of the employee fringe benefit program, i.e., provides insurance certificates, processes claims, ensures payments, maintains records, and prepares reports. Alerts management to problems and opportunities for improvements.
5. Maintains current and accurate position descriptions for all association employees.
6. Administers the compensation program, and alerts management to area wage and salary information and makes recommendations regarding trends and legal compliance.
7. Coordinates the employee performance evaluation process, monitors follow-up activities, and recommends improvements.
8. Maintains personnel files within legal requirements.
9. Maintains and interprets the personnel manual and recommends revisions.
10. Prepares informative reports to staff on benefits and other items of interest; conducts surveys on employee attitudes, and makes recommendations to management.
11. Promotes good employee relations by being accessible for assistance regarding personnel matters as well as consultation on career development and upward mobility.

INTERNAL RELATIONSHIPS:

Reports to the director of administrative services. Has frequent contact with all association employees.

EXTERNAL RELATIONSHIPS:

Has contact with employment agencies, job banks, and other recruiting sources. Contacts government agencies regarding statistics and reports. Contacts insurance agencies and attorneys regarding claims. Has frequent contact with persons in other organizations who have similar responsibilities in personnel administration.

POSITION TITLE: Placement Director

BASIC FUNCTION:

Serves as focal point for information regarding employment of members of the profession, and as employment clearinghouse for members.

SPECIFIC RESPONSIBILITIES:
1. Counsels members, through the association newsletter and individually on request, regarding career planning, career opportunities, and employment application techniques.
2. Solicits information regarding openings and publishes notices in the association newsletter.
3. Furnishes, to organizations placing blind notices of position available, responses submitted by individual members.
4. Assembles and analyzes employment data on members of the profession by location, type of organization, nature of employment, compensation, etc.
5. Prepares an annual report concerning employment, and answers individual questions from members and others.

INTERNAL RELATIONSHIPS:

Reports to the chief staff executive or the deputy chief staff executive. Works occasionally with the publications editor, research director, and membership director.

EXTERNAL RELATIONSHIPS:

Extensive communications with organizations employing members of the profession, with association members, and with sources of information on employment in the profession.

POSITION TITLE: Program Officer

BASIC FUNCTION:

Administer the _____ program of the association.

SPECIFIC RESPONSIBILITIES:
1. Defines program goals and objectives consistent with association policy.
2. Determines the annual program work plan and resource requirements.
3. Trains and supervises program staff.
4. Schedules and coordinates program activities in coordination with association executives and volunteer groups.
5. Evaluates program accomplishments and recommended changes.
6. Analyzes legislative and social developments related to the program.
7. Participates in the association's long range planning and policy development activities.
8. Acts as spokesman for the program to committees, the annual conference, meetings, and in association publications.

INTERNAL RELATIONSHIPS:

Reports to the chief staff executive or the deputy chief staff executive. Frequent contact with other program officers and the directors of publications, government relations, and public relations.

EXTERNAL RELATIONSHIPS:

Has regular contact with representatives of other associations, government agencies, special public interest groups, and national committees.

POSITION TITLE: Director of Publications

BASIC FUNCTION:

Recommends the publishing policies of the association and manages the approved publishing program including editing, advertising, production, and distribution.

SPECIFIC RESPONSIBILITIES:

1. Develops the recommended publications policy of the association and submits for appropriate action.
2. Recommends improvements in the basic format and content of association books, journals, newsletters, periodicals, and brochures.
3. Supervises the editing of publications.
4. Supervises the solicitation of advertising for publications.
5. Ensures that publications are provided according to established policies and procedures.
6. Coordinates the distribution of publications.
7. Maintains current knowledge of publishing techniques.
8. Carries out special publishing projects as required.

INTERNAL RELATIONSHIPS:

Reports to the chief staff executive or the deputy chief staff executive. Frequent contact with the other executives and staff of the association.

EXTERNAL RELATIONSHIPS:

Has regular contact with volunteer officers and committees, representatives of other associations, and other publishing organizations.

POSITION TITLE: Publications Editor

BASIC FUNCTION:

Handles the editorial and production phases of the association's journal, magazine, newsletter, press releases, and other promotional material.

SPECIFIC RESPONSIBILITIES:

1. Develops, in coordination with the membership and advertising functions, a yearly editorial plan.
2. Contacts prospective contributors and arranges for the submission of editorial and photographic material.
3. Analyzes manuscripts so either author or editor can make revisions to reach association editorial standards.
4. Obtains clearances from authors, exercising independent judgement.
5. Analyzes each issue's advertisers and, when required, writes or designs advertising.
6. Arranges typesetting and paste-up of publications and provides clearances.
7. Proofreads galley and page proofs.
8. Contracts for printing and distribution of publication as appropriate.

INTERNAL RELATIONSHIPS:

Reports to the director of publications. Works closely with typesetters, artists, and printers. Has frequent contact with authors and managers of the association.

EXTERNAL RELATIONSHIPS:

Communicates with authors, outside printers, book reviewers, and members of the editorial board.

POSITION TITLE: Public Relations Director

BASIC FUNCTION:

Administers a program to identify the association and its members with the public and builds public support for the association.

SPECIFIC RESPONSIBILITIES:
1. Develops and maintains a theme paper which articulates the desired public image of the association and its members.
2. Writes speeches, press releases, booklets, and scripts.
3. Arranges press coverage of the annual convention.
4. Prepares displays and exhibits for the association's annual convention and other conventions.
5. Answers requests for information from the public.
6. Monitors media coverage of the association, informs the chief staff executive, and recommends responses.
7. Assists association executives and managers to explain to the public the work of specific departments and programs.
8. Advises districts and chapters regarding public relations.

INTERNAL RELATIONSHIPS:

Reports to the chief staff executive or the deputy chief staff executive. Works closely with all of the association's executives and managers and with the elected officers.

EXTERNAL RELATIONSHIPS:

Communicates frequently with newspapers, magazines, journals, radio, and television news contacts. Works with photographers and exhibit contractors.

POSITION TITLE: Regional Office Manager

BASIC FUNCTION:

Provides local membership services and association contact.

SPECIFIC RESPONSIBILITIES:

1. Maintains list of association members in the region.
2. Visits local members to become familiar with their operations and interests, and to promote greater participation in association affairs.
3. Receives member inquiries and ensures prompt response.
4. Serves as extension of headquarters office for regular or special projects, i.e., statistics, research, membership surveys, arranging meetings, employment opportunities, etc.

INTERNAL RELATIONSHIPS:

Reports administratively to the chief staff executive or the deputy chief staff executive. Works with administrative and program staff of the association as appropriate.

EXTERNAL RELATIONSHIPS:

Has regular contact with state and chapter officers and members. Has frequent contact with local businesses and government agencies, business organizations, and the media.

POSITION TITLE: Technical Director

BASIC FUNCTION:

Provides information and advice regarding technical matters affecting the membership and the industry.

SPECIFIC RESPONSIBILITIES:
1. Maintains knowledge of manufacturing processes of members, including equipment and non-proprietary methods.
2. Maintains knowledge of non-proprietary research and development activities of members.
3. Monitors technical needs, both current and projected, of major companies in consumer industries and of government agencies.
4. Monitors technical standards set and proposed by public and private organizations and serves as the association spokesperson regarding those matters.
5. Conducts or sponsors research regarding manufacturing, standards, or other technical matters relating to the industry, the associaton, and its members.
6. Develops articles and news releases for dissemination of information concerning technical matters.
7. Responds to inquiries from members, consumers, government agencies, and others regarding technical matters.

INTERNAL RELATIONSHIPS:

Reports to the chief staff executive or deputy chief staff executive. Works closely with the directors of public relations, government relations, consumer affairs, and information and research.

EXTERNAL RELATIONSHIPS:

Has frequent contact with members, field offices, associations and companies in consumer industries, technical organizations, and government agencies.

POSITION TITLE: Administrative Assistant

BASIC FUNCTION:

Performs a wide variety of detailed and complex administrative tasks with minimum guidance, frequently in a confidential fashion.

SPECIFIC RESPONSIBILITIES:

1. Provides executive secretarial services: takes dictation; handles correspondence; receives and screens calls; makes appointments and travel arrangements; and maintains confidential files.
2. Prepares correspondence independently whenever possible, either composing and sending replies or preparing drafts for the supervisor.
3. Remains aware of those scheduled activities within the division which concern the supervisor, monitors status, provides liaison, and keeps supervisor informed.
4. Compiles and types a variety of reports.
5. Monitors the status of all administrative facets of the division's operations—finance, personnel, furnishings and equipment, and initiates appropriate actions. Acts for the supervisor in related transactions.
6. Conducts research and carries out special administrative projects independently.

INTERNAL RELATIONSHIPS:

Reports to the chief staff executive, deputy chief staff executive, or a division director. Has regular contact on administrative matters with all of the association's managers and other staff.

EXTERNAL RELATIONSHIPS:

Depending on supervisor, has contact with members and various publics, and with outside suppliers of services and materials.

POSITION TITLE: Bookkeeper

BASIC FUNCTION:

Maintains all accounting records, prepares payroll input for processing, and completes other related bookkeeping tasks.

SPECIFIC RESPONSIBILITIES:
1. Prepares statements, bills, reports, and supporting schedules.
2. Prepares journal entries and in collaboration with accountant reconciles inter-fund transfers.
3. Reconciles bank statements.
4. Monitors accounts receivable and initiates follow-up.
5. Drafts regular statements of financial transactions, assets, and liabilities.
6. Prepares payroll input for data processing, and files reports and pays taxes with funds withheld.
7. Serves as custodian of petty cash fund.

INTERNAL RELATIONSHIPS:

Reports to the controller. Works with other association headquarters staff as required.

EXTERNAL RELATIONSHIPS:

Has contact with the association's auditors, government agencies, bank officers, vendors, and computer service bureau.

POSITION TITLE: Clerk-Typist

BASIC FUNCTION:

Performs typing and clerical duties.

SPECIFIC RESPONSIBILITIES:

1. Transcribes dictation from tapes.
2. Types reports, letters, and memoranda from handwritten manuscripts.
3. Maintains files and lists.
4. Substitutes for the receptionist when necessary.

INTERNAL RELATIONSHIPS:

Reports to other department staff as necessary. Works with a department director, an administrative assistant, or a senior secretary.

EXTERNAL RELATIONSHIPS:

Has occasional contact with individual members or chapters regarding requests.

POSITION TITLE: Mail Room Clerk

BASIC FUNCTION:

Receives and distributes incoming mail and dispatches outgoing mail.

SPECIFIC RESPONSIBILITIES:

1. Receives and sorts incoming mail.
2. Distributes mail.
3. Serves as courier for local deliveries and pickups.
4. Stamps outgoing mail.
5. Takes mail and packages to post office.
6. Operates and maintains mailing machine, including record of postage used.
7. Stocks mailing envelopes and related supplies.

INTERNAL RELATIONSHIPS:

Reports to director of administrative services. Has regular contact with secretaries.

EXTERNAL RELATIONSHIPS:

Has frequent contact with postal service personnel and vendors of supplies.

Position Title: Printer

Basic Function:

Operates printing press and related equipment, maintains equipment, and stocks supplies.

Specific Responsibilities:

1. Establishes and maintains day-to-day printing schedules in collaboration with supervisor.
2. Operates and maintains press, folder, and cutter.
3. Receives, inspects, stores, and accounts for paper stock.
4. Maintains inventory of printing supplies and inks.
5. Maintains offset plate and master files.
6. Furnishes camera-ready copy to plate maker when necessary.

Internal Relationships:

Reports to director of publications. Has occasional contact with other staff who request printing.

External Relationships:

Has contact with equipment manufacturers and suppliers.

POSITION TITLE: Receptionist

BASIC FUNCTION:

Operates the telephone switchboard and receives visitors.

SPECIFIC RESPONSIBILITIES:

1. Receives, screens, and routes all calls.
2. Monitors status of telephone equipment and initiates repairs.
3. Maintains a listing of association extension numbers.
4. Performs general typing and clerical tasks.

INTERNAL RELATIONSHIPS:

Reports to the director of administrative services. Has contact with all association staff regarding telephone calls.

EXTERNAL RELATIONSHIPS:

Has extensive telephone contact with the general public. Has regular contact with the telephone company regarding service and repairs.

POSITION TITLE: Secretary (Senior)

BASIC FUNCTION:

Performs administrative and clerical tasks for supervisor.

SPECIFIC RESPONSIBILITIES:
1. Maintains supervisor's calendar and schedules appointments.
2. Takes and screens telephone calls of supervisor.
3. Arranges meeting facilities.
4. Makes travel arrangements.
5. Reviews supervisor's mail, attaches appropriate files, and drafts answers to routine correspondence.
6. Takes dictation and transcribes notes on typewriter, and transcribes voice recordings.
7. Compiles and types statistical reports.
8. Establishes and maintains files.

INTERNAL RELATIONSHIPS:

Reports to a department manager or other supervisor. Has frequent contact with association staff with whom supervisor works.

EXTERNAL RELATIONSHIPS:

Has frequent contact with members and other individuals and organizations with whom the supervisor communicates.

POSITION TITLE: Secretary (Junior)

BASIC FUNCTION:

Performs administrative and clerical tasks for department staff.

SPECIFIC RESPONSIBILITIES:

1. Types correspondence and reports.
2. Receives and relays messages for absent department staff.
3. Makes travel arrangements.
4. Maintains files.
5. Substitutes for the receptionist when necessary.

INTERNAL RELATIONSHIPS:

Reports to a department director and works with the entire department staff.

EXTERNAL RELATIONSHIPS:

Has occasional contact with membership regarding assigned department area.

Chapter V

STAFF COMPENSATION

Chapters III and IV discussed the organization of association functions and staff and the definition and documentation of responsibilities. The next element in this sequence of management steps is the development of an appropriate method of compensation for the staff who perform those responsibilities.

For the purpose of this discussion, compensation is defined as salary and any benefits provided to staff in return for their work in the association. The compensation may be based on a straight salary or an hourly wage rate. In most associations all fulltime staff—both exempt and non-exempt—are paid on a straight salary basis. Benefits include both absorbed benefits such as holidays, vacation, and sick leave, and paid benefits such as insurance, payment of educational fees, and parking allowances.

Compensation is a critical part of management. Not only is some form of salary administration required simply to hire and maintain the staff, it is also a valuable management tool for motivating and directing staff and for focusing the association's resources. Given the high cost of labor today, the association executive must have a sound process for administering salary and benefits to ensure effective management of the organization's financial resources.

There is no perfect solution for handling compensation issues; no ideal salary administration system exists. To be truly effective, a compensation program must be tailored to address the needs of the organization in which it is used. Organizations are too diverse and too complex to enable the development of a single system or process which will satisfy all the possible requirements. For these reasons, this chapter does not recommend a particular system for salary and benefits administration. Instead, it raises a number of the important issues which are relevant to compensation management. The chapter presents some general principles of compensation and discusses a variety of approaches for administering salaries in the association environment.

Salary Administration is Part of a Compensation Program

Any system for establishing salaries should take into consideration the value of benefits. These two elements, salaries and benefits, should complement each other and reflect the management philosophy of the association and be tailored to meet its needs. An association may wish to attract and retain young employees which it has found are interested primarily in the highest salary levels they can achieve. Therefore, the association's management may decide to pay high salaries and provide modest benefits. Another association may determine that its staff members prefer to receive a significant portion of their compensation in nontaxable benefits. Whatever the appropriate allocation may be, the association should carefully assess these issues in designing its compensation program.

Generally, the administration and maintenance of the salary program is far more difficult and complex than management of the benefits program. As a result, a variety of salary administration systems have been devised. Many of these systems will be discussed later in the chapter. First, it is necesssary to review some of the issues which underlie compensation and salary administration theories.

Underlying Issues for Compensation

Associations are service organizations and rely solely on people for the delivery of their services. Therefore, the effective direction and motivation of association staff is one of the most important factors in determining the association's success. Compensation is a major element of human resource management. In addressing the subject of compensation, it is important to explore some of the basic underlying economic and psychological issues. There are some principles of economics and behavioral science which should be understood in the context of their implications for effective salary administration.

Economic Issues

Compensation is clearly an element in the economics of an association's management. Even in an association with a small staff, economic conditions and trends are relevant to salary administration. The internal financial posture is the economic factor which is of most direct concern. But salary administration is affected by many external economic forces as well. Associations are service organizations created to address the collective and, sometimes, individual needs of members of an industry or profession. The ability and willingness of the members to support the association through dues or purchase of special services is directly related to economic conditions which affect them. Those conditions may be determined by situations within the industry or profession the association serves or they may be driven by national—or even international—economic trends.

In designing and maintaining a salary administration program, the association executive or other appropriate staff must be aware of economic factors. It will be relevant to assess current economic conditions and anticipate future trends. What is happening in the economy today and what is likely to happen? Each association must look at its own special circumstances. Does the economy of the association's industry or profession reflect national economic trends? Is it tied to private sector business activities or public sector spending? Many of these factors determine not only whether the association will be able to support a growing compensation program for current staff, but also whether the staff is likely to grow because of requirements for new services. All of these elements have implications for the salary administration program. The association should be aware of as many variables as possible in designing or maintaining a system.

Another economic aspect of salary administration is the need to design a system which will encourage productivity among staff members and motivate them to seek maximum effectiveness and efficiency in the utilization of the association's resources. The system should support performance which will contribute to the growth of the association.

In summary, the association executive or other staff member responsible for the association's compensation program must be aware of the economic factors which affect the organization and the relationship of the program to the overall financial status of the association. Salary administration must be viewed as a part of the management and control process and not as an appendage to it.

Behavioral Issues

It is important to keep in mind relevant psychological or behavioral principles when designing and administering a salary administration program.

There is a theory that "money does not motivate." It has been cited to indicate the futility of trying to tie compensation to performance and, in some cases, to avoid the effort required to develop an effective, tailored salary administration program. The statement has validity in some cases. But it is also a sweeping generality which must be taken in context. Clearly, there are times and situations in which money does motivate. Persons of dissimilar backgrounds and ages are often motivated by different factors. In administering compensation programs, it is important to be aware of these differences and to address them.

In order to understand these differences it is useful to consider some behavioral and historical theories. One of the most relevant behavioral theories is Maslow's hierarchy of needs theory. According to Maslow, people have five levels of need. The first is a basic physiological need—the need for food and shelter. Security is the second level. Once these needs are satisfied, people attempt to fulfill their third level of needs—social needs—which are manifested in the desire for acceptance, love, and affection. After meeting those needs, people seek ego satisfaction—the fourth level of needs—through achievement of positions of power and authority, and distinction among peers. Finally, the last level of need is self-actualization or self-fulfillment. There is a clear distinction between ego satisfaction and self-fulfillment. For ego satisfaction people seek recognition from outside, from peers and superiors. But in self-actualization, the reward is internal and may result in no external recognition.

The important point of the hierarchy of needs is that each need must be satisfied before a person seeks the fulfillment of the next need in the hierarchy. And just as significant is the assertion that when the satisfaction of the basic need is removed or challenged, the whole hierarchy comes down, and the person has to rebuild from the bottom once again. Thus, the theory presents a balanced, fragile view of the human ability to achieve complete fulfillment.

Some experts theorize that the environment in which people have grown up will affect the way in which they respond to Maslow's hierarchy of needs. People who grew up in environments influenced by the Depression, who actually experienced periods of want or who were cautioned constantly by parents to be frugal and avoid want, are said to be more concerned about basic needs.

Younger people who grew up in an environment of material wealth, and who have not experienced want, are motivated by the needs at the higher levels of Maslow's hierarchy. But at certain times or under certain conditions even persons in this group are motivated by a basic need such as money. When they have families of their own they must provide the basic staples for survival, and there is pressure to provide luxury items as well. Under these requirements, money becomes a motivating factor.

If one considers Maslow's hierarchy of needs in conjunction with the average person's reaction to money, it is possible to analyze the motivation factor of money. As long as a person's income is not lower than his expenditures, the "break-even" point is not reached. During this period, a person is likely to put forth a reasonable amount of effort for a reasonable amount of pay. When the need for money is greater than the amount of money coming in, a person will work harder with money as a motivating factor. After the break-even point in income and expenditure is reached, a person's effort is likely to level off and to require more money for greater motivation. In short, more money is required when a person perceives that he or she is trying to satisfy social needs; then the survival factor is no longer a prevailing concern. In Maslow's theory, increased income is considered an ego satisfier since it recognizes achievement among peers and reflects attainment of power and authority. When a person is engaged in activity that results in self-actualization, however, he or she is likely to work harder without an increase in salary. As already noted, the younger employees, whose formative years were not influenced by the Depression, generally have lower "survival requirements" or basic needs. As a result, they usually seek self-actualization sooner than their older colleagues.

For the purpose of salary administration, the association executive or other appropriate administrator should be aware of these psychological theories and the likely differences in responses among various age groups. In designing a system, the association should assess its staff in terms of age, performance levels, and ability or skill level. The system should be able to motivate employees with different needs and different levels of needs.

Another important behavioral factor to consider in administering compensation is the staff's perception of the program and the related procedures. Even if the program is carefully developed and is designed to address broad employee needs, it will not be successful if the staff has a negative perception of it.

To avoid this situation some associations involve staff in the design and evolution of the salary administration system. A staff task force may be created to work with the association executive or another representative of management. There are a number of possible advantages inherent in this design method.

- **Improved communications.** The involvement of the staff in the design process can establish an important link and communication channel between the association's management and staff at all levels.
- **Staff appreciation for problems of salary administration.** Participating in this process, staff members become aware of the sensitivities and difficulties involved in developing and maintaining an equitable salary program.
- **Quality of resulting program.** In these situations, the staff tends to be very basic and logical in its thinking. Employees realize that their work on the task force is open to the scrutiny of their peers and their supervisors. Therefore, the program which results from the task force's efforts is usually very basic and workable. It is then easy to implement within the association, and, as a result, is less costly and less time-consuming than complex programs. The simplicity of the program facilitates its ongoing administration.
- **Acceptance is high.** When the staff is involved in developing the program, acceptance of the final product is high. When the staff as a whole understands that colleagues and peer representatives are par-

ticipating in the design, each individual is comfortable that his views can be heard. The staff then usually has a higher commitment to making the system work when it is actually implemented. For these reasons the association should communicate the task force's role and purpose to the staff through a meeting, a memorandum, or a newsletter. And the staff should be given a mechanism to contribute views on compensation to the members of the task force.

There are some basic guidelines that should be followed in creating the task force:

- The members of the task force should be selected, *not* elected. If they are elected by their peers, the members may feel compelled to "represent their interests" and take a partisan approach to the problem. Task force members should be selected to represent all levels of the association's staff.
- Management must maintain control over the task force. Involvement of the staff does not displace the responsibility or authority of the association's chief staff executive or other members of the executive staff. Therefore, actual selection of the task force members should be done by the association executive or other appropriate management staff, depending on the size and organization of the association staff as a whole. This method is appropriate since the chief staff executive is ultimately responsible for the association and its administrative policies.

What is a Salary System?

There are all types of salary systems and approaches to salary administration. However, the logic used in each is essentially the same. First the association does an analysis of its staff jobs. After this study, the association's management must decide what factors should be used to place particular positions in the overall hierarchy of jobs, and thus to determine the salary level. A system is then designed to evaluate all staff positions on the basis of these factors. This system and the evaluation process are used to establish an appropriate hierarchy which includes all association staff positions. Finally, specific salary levels, or ranges, are assigned to the jobs within the hierarchy.

The American Society of Association Executives (ASAE) offers a Salary Administration Service that is tailored to the specialized needs of associations. It is designed to help associations set up and maintain a system with minimal disruption of the asociation work flow, although it does require some time committment and the dedication of senior staff executives.

When Does an Association Need a Salary System?

Most associations begin small. Some start with a staff executive and one or two other staff. Clearly, at this stage of development, the association does not need a formal salary "system." However, even the small association (with less than five staff positions) should have a systematic approach for determining salary levels and awarding salary increases.

- As a matter of practice, the staff executive or other designated staff member should gather salary data from comparable organizations to ensure that salaries are based on those paid by other similar associations.
- Procedures should exist to ensure internal and external equity in staff salaries.
- The association executive should have guidelines for ensuring fairness and consistency in the award of salary increases. Ideally, merit increases should be based directly on a regular formal staff performance appraisal. The issues of "cost-of-living" and "longevity" compensation should be addressed through a formal policy, and should be clearly separated from considerations of merit.

Thus, although associations with small staffs would be overwhelmed and overburdened by the administrative requirements and costs involved with a formal salary system, they would realize many advantages from a systematic approach to the salary administration process. Experience has shown that established policies and procedures help to remove subjectivity in salary decisions and thereby reduce management problems, avoid charges of inequitable treatment, and prevent confusion among staff.

These same advantages are relevant in associations with larger staffs. However, as the staff gets larger (15 or more) and usually more diverse, it becomes more difficult to distinguish levels of positions and to ensure internal equitability in salaries. It is frequently at this time that an association considers adopting a formal salary system—specifically a system for evaluating staff positions and a formal pay structure based on the evaluations.

Job evaluation is a critical element in the personnel program. A good system has many benefits.

- An evaluation system defines the scope and responsibilities of jobs.
- The clarity which results from the evaluation process can help to prevent job overlap and duplication.
- The definition of responsibilities provides a basis for refining the functional organization of the association.
- The process of job evaluation can support effective human resources planning. When job responsibilities and qualifications are clearly defined, the association can hire more effectively—finding the appropriate person for each job.
- Job evaluation provides a sound basis for performance appraisal.

Once the scope, responsibilities, and qualifications are clearly defined, the basis for performance appraisal becomes more objective.

Clearly, if an association with a staff of more than 15 different staff positions does not have a systematic procedure for position evaluation, it should take steps to establish one. The need to revise the association's existing process is less clear cut. But there are a number of situations which serve as indicators that the association needs to revise its system for evaluating staff positions and creating a supporting staff salary structure.

- **Too many job descriptions.** If the association has an inordinately large number of distinct position descriptions, it is likely that the existing process for evaluation is too complex and detailed.
- **Job descriptions are not up to date.** Few positions remain completely stable in an association. In fact, most are changing constantly in response to internal and external factors. Updating of job descriptions often lags significantly behind these changes because the process is time-consuming and complicated. As already noted in Chapter IV, it is important to develop simple job descriptions and then establish an uncomplicated procedure for updating them. If position descriptions have not been revised for a long period of time, the need for a new method of position evaluation will be proportionately higher.
- **Compensation factors are not relevant.** Changes in the association and in the staff positions often require changes in the compensation factors—those factors which are used to evaluate a position and determine its salary in relation to salaries for other positions in the organization. If these factors are not reassessed periodically in relation to the jobs and to the changes which are occurring, they may cease to measure the value of the jobs. In some cases, factors may not have been appropriate when the system was adopted. They may have been selected initially because they were used by other organizations. But they may not actually measure what is important to the association and thus not measure the job's contribution to the association. When jobs are priced wrong, when the market value of certain jobs is higher than the association's salary levels, it is also likely that there will be a problem with the compensation factors. Several options are usually followed when this situation occurs. The job may be redefined to get a higher evaluation. The evaluation may simply be changed, thereby compromising the system. Or the job can be pulled out of the system as an anomaly. None of these options are really acceptable. It is more appropriate to revise the compensation factors. The problem may be that the factors focus on activities performed by the job and not the contribution the job makes to the association.
- **Turnover problems exist.** Certainly, there may be a number of circumstances that contribute to turnover problems. But one of them

may be inappropriate compensation levels. Too low a rate of turnover may be as much a problem as too high a rate of staff turnover. Generally, some turnover is good in an association, and too much or too little usually indicates a problem. Some turnover is healthy because it can indicate that the association is staffed by dynamic and growing people—ones who move on to greater challenges after making their contributions. Also, it helps to ensure that the association has an opportunity for exposure to new, fresh ideas. Without some turnover, the association may accept the status quo, stagnate, and cease to grow and develop. High turnover may be due to "undercompensation." Low turnover may be related to "overcompensation."
- **System becomes mired in paperwork.** Over a period of years, an evaluation system can become extremely complicated and burdensome and must be supported by an inordinate amount of paperwork. This type of system creates a bureaucratic environment which is not beneficial for the association. In such cases, the system should be replaced by a simple position evaluation process.
- **Inordinate increase in payroll costs.** When the evaluation system and supporting salary structure do not provide adequate control over staff salaries, payroll costs may escalate. In those circumstances, staff salaries may account for an inappropriate proportion of the association budget. This situation may indicate that a new system is needed to bring about the required control.

Tailoring the System to the Association

Once the association determines that a salary administration system is needed or that an existing system should be revised, it must decide which system it should adopt. Generally, there are no simple answers, no hard and fast rules to guide the association in this decision. As noted at the outset of this chapter, methods for salary and benefits administration must be tailored to an organization. It is unlikely that a system which works well in one association will work just as well in another and meet all the needs of that organization. The association should look at its particular characteristics and requirements and evolve a program which will meet its particular needs. There are a number of relevant factors for determining the approach an association should follow.

- **The organization's style.** Both the management and operating styles should be considered. Is the association's style formal or informal?
- **The size of the association staff.** The approach that is right for an association with a large staff may not be appropriate for the small association.
- **The nature of the services performed by the association.** If the organization's primary service is government relations, it may require a somewhat different method than if its primary purpose is to pub-

lish and distribute written materials to its members. Similarly, if the association's focus is on the delivery of member services through a complex regionalized organization, it will require a special approach for administering staff salaries.
- **Employee numbers and skill levels.** This characteristic is related to the nature of the services the association provides, since that factor dictates to some degree the type of staff the association must hire. If the staff is composed primarily of technical specialists, salary administration procedures will be different than if the staff is almost totally clerical.
- **Locale of the organization.** The locale of the association and the nature of the surrounding organizations with which it must compete for staff are important in determining an association's approach to salary administration.

There are also some general guidelines which should be considered in designing or selecting a system.

- **Objectivity.** The system should ensure objectivity in the evaluation of jobs and the determination of salary levels.
- **Simplicity.** The methods and procedures for the system should be as simple as possible.
- **Clarity.** The system should be clear and understandable to all staff. The rationale and principles should be logical and realistic.
- **Meaningfulness.** The process for evaluating positions and administering salaries should be meaningful to all association staff. If the staff cannot associate the compensation factors in the system with their salaries, they will not be motivated to perform to their capacity.
- **Ease in development and administration.** The salary administration system should be easy to develop and administer. Some systems require long and complicated position descriptions and specifications. As a result, those systems also require considerable time to develop and administer. In many cases, the association finds it needs an additional person or persons just to develop and maintain such a system. An association should strive for as simple a system as possible.
- **Cost.** If the system is complex and difficult to manage and maintain, then the administrative costs involved will be high. A simple system will require less investment of staff time and will thus be less costly for the association.
- **Flexibility.** A good system will be flexible. It should be able to accommodate reorganization of the association staff and both vertical and horizontal growth in the organizational structure. In short, the system should remain relevant for the association even if it undergoes a significant amount of change.

Types of Position Evaluation Systems

There are three main types of position evaluation systems which are commonly used in organizations: (1) ranking, (2) classification, and (3) point. Each of these systems is described below.

Ranking System

Ranking is the simplest and easiest method of job evaluation. Even organizations which say they do not have a system for evaluation actually employ an informal ranking process. There is always a "pecking order" of job hierarchy. The association pays more for some jobs than others and someone has to determine the value of each job.

In a ranking system, the association's staff positions are ranked from highest to lowest in terms of the whole job or the overall job complexity and responsibilities. This ranking process is relatively easy if there is a limited number of staff positions. However, it can become quite cumbersome if there are many different positions on the association staff.

There are other disadvantages which limit the usefulness of the ranking system. Different individuals doing the ranking may use different bases for comparison if there are not specific standards for evaluating the positions. Thus the hierarchy of jobs may vary from rater to rater. Specific job requirements such as responsibility, knowledge, skill, and impact are not usually analyzed separately in the ranking process. Frequently, the rater's judgement is influenced by the existing salary levels—even though an overall reevaluation of positions may be undertaken. Further, the ranking system does not provide a mechanism or procedure for substantiating or justifying the ranking.

The entire process is subjective. The ranking method is nonquantitative and involves an ordinary numbering scale. As a result, the ranking system does not distinguish the distance between jobs in terms of their complexity and levels of responsibility. For example, the first three jobs in the hierarchy of staff positions might be clearly distinguishable in terms of overall responsibility and difficulty. But the next three positions might cluster together and be very similar in level of difficulty. The nature of the ranking method may wrongly indicate that the differences between jobs are essentially equivalent.

The primary virtue of the ranking system is that it is easy to implement and administer. But this situation is true only as long as the association staff does not include more than 15 or 20 different positions.

Classification System

The position classification system is also referred to as a grade description system. Under this system, the hierarchy of positions is divided into a number of grades or salary groups. Written definitions are prepared for each grade and all staff positions are assigned to a particular grade classification. The grade definitions are developed on the basis of information derived from job analysis. After the formulation and analysis of job descriptions and job specifications, all jobs are grouped into classes or grades that represent different salary levels ranging from low to high. Common types of responsibilities, knowledge, and skills should be identified through the process of job analysis.

As a result of this process, jobs with similar requirements are grouped in a common grade or classification. Then grade descriptions are written for each job classification (group of staff positions). After this framework is set, the grade descriptions can be used as a standard for assigning all positions in the association to a particular salary grade.

The position classification system is an extension of the ranking method, involving a larger number of positions. General position classifications and grades are established and then ranked in relationship to one another (grade 1, grade 2, grade 3, etc.). Specific positions are assigned to particular grades and are usually ranked in relationship to other positions.

The classification system can be considered an improvement over the ranking system since it calls for a more thorough analysis of jobs. Classification of positions requires more extensive and careful analysis. This process helps to identify and solve many salary administration problems. The grade descriptions which result from the classification are used as fixed written standards or guides against which to analyze the association staff positions. The groupings of positions into classes helps to reduce problems involved in salary determination. Salary levels or ranges are determined and assigned to all position classifications. The classification method can be applied effectively in associations that range widely in staff size—from as few as 20 to as many as a few hundred.

There are a number of disadvantages in the classification method of position evaluation. Grade descriptions must, of necessity, be general and abstract in order to encompass a number of different jobs. Also, like the ranking system, position classification depends on an ordinal scale which is nonquantitative in format. Thus, there are no equal differences in job responsibility between position grades or classifications. Also, the grade descriptions in this system do not provide a means for weighting the compensable factors that make up the staff positions. To avoid these disadvantages, many associations use a point system or factor comparison system.

Point System

The point system is widely used by associations that have formal position evaluation systems. Point systems may follow a standard format or they may be uniquely tailored to the association. However, all these systems require a set of job factors or characteristics for determining compensation levels. Industrial point systems have commonly utilized four main job factor sets: skill, effort, responsibility, and job conditions. These factors vary somewhat in the point systems used by associations. Job conditions are usually not relevant to association positions.

Each of the basic job factor sets usually contains numerous elements or subsets of factors. For example, skill may be subdivided into judgment, adaptability, experience, and so forth. Responsibility can be broken into subfactors such as number of subordinates and total budget. No single point system utilizes all the possible subfactors. Instead, each plan selects roughly eight to twelve characteristics that best apply to the organization in which positions are being analyzed. These characteristics generally vary from association to association depending on the nature of its activities.

Each factor is then subdivided into degrees that define the relative extent and amount of that factor that is required for the association positions. As an example, experience might be subdivided into five degrees: first degree, less than one year; second degree, one to three years; third degree, three to five years; fourth degree, five to ten years; and fifth degree, over ten years. Written definitions are prepared for each degree. A precise set scale of points is assigned to the degrees of each factor.

When each staff position is evaluated, the proper degree for each and all factors is determined and the respective point values are added to obtain a final total position score. This total is tied to a certain pay level which represents an exact salary range. When point totals from the point matrix have been determined, a point conversion table, as shown below, is used to translate position points into salary dollars.

Point Range	Salary Range
101-150	$ 7,500- 9,000
151-200	9,000-11,000
201-250	11,000-14,000
251-300	14,000-17,500
301-350	17,500-23,000
351-400	23,000-27,500
401-450	27,500-31,000
451-500	31,000-35,000

The point system is clearly more complex than the classification system. Only one scale is needed to classify positions, but numerous scales are required for the point system of position evaluation. In many systems, a separate scale must be created for each of the eight to twelve compensation factors. Each of the job factors and factor degrees must be defined precisely, and all the definitions must be phrased in words that reflect subjective human judgment—which still must be applied even in a point system. Although the point system gives the impression of being objective, it is still dependent upon subjective decisions.

As with all evaluation systems, there are a number of advantages and disadvantages inherent in the point system. One advantage is the stability of the rating scales. Once the scales are developed, they may be used for an extended period of time. And, if properly developed at the outset, these scales are generally reliable and valid. Staff members tend to react favorably to the point system of evaluation because it is more systematic and objective than the other possible systems. Also, salary ranges for specific positions are easy to determine from the total position point values. Finally, the point system provides clear substantiation of the position evaluations and creation of the position hierarchy.

The greatest disadvantage of the point system is the cost required to develop and implement an effective point system. The task of properly defining job factors and factor degrees can be immensely time-consuming and difficult. Considerable clerical work is required to record and summarize the rating scales, especially if a number of raters are involved in the process. Because of the complexity and unique features of a point system, staff members may find it difficult and confusing.

Despite these drawbacks, many associations use a point system for position evaluation because it provides greater accuracy. However, due to the complexity of a point system and the time and cost required for development and implementation, the system is not recommended for associations with small staffs. But the system is probably justified if there are at least 20 different positions on the staff.

Establishing a Salary Structure

The evaluation process sets the framework for the salary structure, creating a hierarchy for salary levels. But the association must still determine appropriate salary levels. The determination of salaries is generally now considered a logical, consistent, and systematic process. There are many factors or standards which are used to determine salary levels. Usually, several factors rather than a single factor determine the salary levels. The criteria which are used by associations are usually partly economic and partly behavioral, consistent with the principles discussed earlier in this chapter. The most common criteria are: (1) comparable salary levels, (2) ability to pay, and (3) cost of living. Each of these criteria is addressed briefly.

- **Comparable salary levels.** Comparable or prevailing salary levels are the most influential of all the salary criteria. Most associations determine their salary levels by assessing the levels paid by other similar associations. The association's management determines whether the association's salary levels will be high, average, or low in comparison with the levels paid by other associations or other organizations with whom it must compete for staff. Some associations pay on the high side in an attempt to create good will among staff or to ensure an adequate supply of qualified personnel. Other associ-

ations pay on the low side simply because they cannot afford to pay more.
- **Ability to pay.** The ability of the association to pay affects the general compensation levels and structure. The size of an association's budget and the organization's financial well-being is without question a consideration in determining overall salary levels. Ability to pay seldom determines precise salary ranges. Instead, it sets the range within which overall salaries are fixed.
- **Cost of living.** This compensation criterion calls for salary adjustments based on increases in the official cost of living index. In some associations this factor is addressed when setting the overall salary scale. In others it is considered separately from basic salary levels and salary increases for merit or longevity.

Administering Salary Ranges

Once the salary levels or ranges are set for each level of positions or class (grade) of positions, or point range, the association must determine how it will administer salaries within the ranges. Regardless of the evaluation system used, most associations which have formal evaluation systems have systematic procedures for moving a staff member upward within the salary range. Some associations recognize and reward longevity in positions. But the primary approach is to reward staff for meritorious performance.

In granting these rewards the association generally uses one of the following approaches.
- A salary table is used which has a range and specific step increases for each grade or level of positions. Each staff member is placed on the salary table when the system is implemented. The individual salary is then advanced upward step by step on the basis of merit, or if applicable, longevity. In instances of exceptional performance, more than one step increase may be granted.
- A range is set for each level or grade of positions or each set of points. General guidelines are established and the individual supervisors are allowed to recommend increases for staff within the set ranges. The increases may also be based on merit or on longevity.
- Specific ranges are set for each level or grade of position. Management establishes a specific percentage of increase for various levels of performance. In this approach the supervisor has less flexibility.

Any approach which provides for merit increases must be supported by a sound performance appraisal system. Ideally, formal performance appraisals should be conducted each year as a basis for determining merit increases.

A system for merit increases is usually more effective if it is clearly distinguished from cost of living or longevity increases. When cost of living adjustments are handled separately, each salary range, and each step on a salary table if a salary table is used, is adjusted upward by a set percentage which is determined by the association's management.

Chapter VI

PERSONNEL MANAGEMENT

This chapter explores important aspects of personnel management which enhance the effectiveness of the association's staff organization. It includes sections on staffing, personnel recordkeeping, training and development, and performance appraisal.

Staffing

Staffing includes the variety of activities required to ensure that the association maintains a qualified, effective staff. It includes the recruitment, selection, hiring, and orientation of persons to fill staff positions. Since the staff is the key to the association's success, the staffing functions must be effective.

In some situations, associations may be able to recruit internally. Internal recruitment is beneficial for two reasons. The association already has first-hand knowledge of the individual's performance ability and loyalty. Also, promotions are a boost to overall employee morale because they provide an incentive to other staff members in the form of opportunity for upward mobility. Posting available jobs, in a central location, with all the relevant information (position title, salary, duties and responsibilities, eligibility requirements) is an excellent method of ensuring that all who are qualified have the chance to apply. Sometimes an association may decide simply to review personnel records and reward a competent employee by making a direct job offer, without opening the position to competition.

External recruitment can be conducted through ASAE, private employment agencies, public employment agencies, college placement offices, or advertising. If the association decides to advertise a vacant position, there are other resources available in addition to the local newspaper. Professional journals and other association newsletters are valuable tools for external recruitment, particularly when the association is searching for a person with a specific skill or type of work experience.

Whichever method is used to recruit personnel, certain restraints must be exercised. Federal regulations concerning equal employment opportunities and affirmative action must be considered and steps must be taken to ensure nondiscriminatory hiring practices. State laws must also be considered when developing association recruitment policies. Policy statements concerning hiring practices should cover social responsibility for the employment of minorities and the disadvantaged.

An association should coordinate its recruitment activities with its selection procedures. An association which spends large amounts of money recruiting hundreds of applicants only to select one or two is wasting resources. The selection process can be time-consuming and costly. Some associations use what is referred to as the "successive hurdles" approach to hiring. Each applicant must fulfill all the requirements of each step to proceed to the next. Only by successfully completing all the hurdles can an applicant be considered for the job. With "compensating selection," a deficiency in one area can be offset by a strength in another area. The association must weigh the job requirements and score an applicant accordingly. A variety of instruments may be used in selecting employees, and they may be used individually or in combination with each other.

Applications

Applications serve as the initial source of information about the applicant. They provide data on the background and qualifications of an individual in an efficient, accessible form. There is no general consensus among experts on what information should be included on an application. Federal and state laws prohibit the requesting of data on race, religion, age, sex, and marital status. Each association must tailor its applications to its own needs and hiring requirements while ensuring that all legal restrictions are observed. A generally acceptable employment application form follows this chapter as *Exhibit VI-A*.

Testing

Extensive testing is generally used only by very large associations. The primary use of tests in most associations is to measure skill levels for clerical, typing, shorthand, and other office machines. In response to government pressure to validate tests, many associations have abandoned the use of testing rather than expend the time and resources required for the validation process. There are several types of tests which can be used for selection of employees.

Aptitude Tests measure an individual's potential ability to perform. There are aptitude tests such as I.Q. tests which measure general intelligence and there are also aptitude tests geared to measure a specific skill such as typing, dexterity, perception, mechanical ability, or sales.

Achievement Tests measure an achieved skill or acquired knowledge which is usually the result of training, education, or work experience. These tests can be used to assess an individual's job knowledge.

Vocational Interest Inventories are lists of likes and dislikes related to an individual's occupation, hobbies, and recreational interests. The assumption is that there are definite patterns of interest for people who are successful in a certain occupation. These tests are used mainly for vocational guidance, not hiring, as it is possible for the respondent to adjust the answers to what he or she thinks is expected.

When using any type of testing, there are certain factors which should be considered.

1. *Tests should only be used as a supplement to other information.* They should not be viewed as the absolute indicator of success or failure on a job. Tests should be used only as a preliminary or screening device in the process.
2. *Tests have been shown to be better at indicating failure than success in a position.* Test results assess who will not perform well on a job, rather than who will have a superior job performance.
3. *Test scores are not precise.* A 90 percent testing score does not mean that the applicant will perform on the job with 90 percent efficiency.
4. *Tests should be validated or tested before use in the environment in which they will be administered.* Validity refers to the degree to which the test measures what it is intended to measure. A test should also be reliable and consistent. An individual should receive the same score each time he or she takes the test providing there has been no intervening educational or training procedure.

Interviews

The interview is essential to any association staffing procedure. It involves verbal interaction between an applicant and one or more members of the association staff, and it provides an opportunity to discuss the application form, test results, and other screening devices. The interview should be a two-way process, so that while the association is accumulating information about the applicant, the applicant is gathering information about the association from the interviewer.

There are three interview formats described below which may be tailored to the association's needs and the preference of the interviewer.

The *planned interview* is partially structured in advance, so that the interviewer knows what questions to ask and what information should be acquired. Questions usually involve education, work experience, attitudes, and interests. The applicant receives information on the organization, services provided, salary, opportunities for advancement, and job demands.

The *directed interview* is rigidly structured, usually involving a printed, detailed questionnaire.

A *stress interview* is used for jobs which are considered to be highly stressful in the requirements and the working environment. The interviewer assumes the role of an interrogator and seeks to annoy, embarrass, and frustrate the applicant. The results indicate how well the applicant can withstand a pressured situation.

In any interview format, the applicant and interviewer should do equal amounts of talking. The interviewer can facilitate this process by asking open-ended questions which require more than yes or no answers.

An interviewer should also be aware of possible pitfalls in the process. One is a failure to listen well. Above all, the interviewer should be attentive to ensure that the information is digested and remembered. Another possible problem is a "halo effect," where the interviewer makes specific assumptions about an individual based on one or more visible characteristics. For example, the halo effect occurs when the interviewer attributes to the applicant the characteristics of intelligence, dependability, and maturity, based purely on physical appearance.

Studies of the interview process have resulted in some interesting conclusions that should be considered when using interview results for staffing.

1. *The intra-rater reliability is high for interviews.* If the same interviewer questions an applicant more than one time, he or she will reach the same conclusions each time.
2. *Inter-rater reliability is low if it is not a highly structured interview.* Different interviewers will reach different conclusions about the same applicant.
3. *A high assessment interview is not necessarily indicative of high performance on a job.*
4. *Team interviews can increase the validity of an interview.* With more than one person asking the questions, chances are higher of receiving information relevant to job performance.
5. *The results of an interview are strongly based on the attitudes and biases of the interviewer.*
6. *Interviews are primarily a search for negative information.* An interviewer is more likely to remember negative characteristics than positive ones.
7. *Interviewers generally make their final decisions early in the process.* First appearances are the basis of their decisions and can set the tone for the remainder of the interview, especially with an unstructured format.

8. *In an unstructured interview the interviewer will talk more than the applicant.* When using this format, precautions should be taken to prevent this situation from occurring.

Staff Orientation

An integral part of the staffing process is the orientation of the new employee to the position. This process generally involves a period of adjustment during which an employee forms attitudes, begins to feel a sense of belonging, and is motivated to perform. Indoctrination can be too structured and can result in conformity that stifles creative thought.

A good orientation program involves a general introduction to the organization before the training in specific job skills begins. The new employee should receive information about association services, introductions to co-workers, a tour of the office and explanations of employee benefits, salary policies, general rules of conduct, training and development opportunities, and performance evaluations. An effective staff orientation program can result in reduced learning time, a higher output, better attendance, improved quality of performance, and a lower level of anxiety and stress in new employees.

Personnel Recordkeeping

The maintenance of accurate personnel records is a necessity for every association. A personnel file should be maintained for each employee. It should include:
- personal information (name, address, phone number, person to contact in case of emergency, birthdate)
- date of hire, test results if tests are used
- dates on all personnel actions (promotions, reprimands, etc.)
- dates and results of all performance appraisals
- salary history with dates of each increase, history of training and development (dates and nature of all activities)
- work experience
- educational background
- qualifications.

The record may also contain special information such as employee interests, languages spoken, special skills, etc. It is critical that all information in the personnel files remain strictly confidential. Only authorized personnel should have access to the records, and the number of authorized personnel should be limited to only those that have a specific need for the information, i.e., the personnel officer if one exists, or the staff member who prepare payrolls. Each association will utilize a different recordkeeping system depending on the size of staff and the capacity of the personnel office. Many large associations have found computerization to be an effective method for storing personnel information. Computerized records make it easier to incorporate a wide range of facts and descriptive data for each employee. Associations without the resources for a computerized system may rely on written files. As with a more sophisticated method, it is essential that all material be kept up-to-date, so that the files are always accurate.

Whether an association uses computerized or written records, the most important factor is that the information be easily accessible for use. If data is difficult to obtain, then the purpose of personnel records is defeated. There should be several staff members who are thoroughly familiar with the operation of the system, so that they can respond quickly to requests for information.

Staff Training and Development

The emphasis on staff training and development has greatly increased in recent years, and will continue to do so in the 1980s. Many association executives now view training as a long-term investment in human resources rather than as an unnecessary expense.

A definite distinction can be made between training and development. Training is generally a short-term educational process that is systematically organized and aimed at non-supervisory personnel. It has a narrow purpose which is usually the acquisition of specific manual and operational skills.

Development usually pertains to managerial-level personnel, and is a longer term process than training. Development activities are designed to provide general knowledge and often involve abstract and theoretical concepts.

Purpose of Training and Development

Since associations have different staffing patterns, their training needs will differ accordingly. But all associations will find that an effective training and development program can benefit not only the individual recipient, but the organization as a whole, through increased staff efficiency and competence. Adequate training can reduce the amount of time necessary for an employee to reach an acceptable level of performance in a new position, or it may improve an employee's performance in a current job. The increase in individual effectiveness will result in an overall rise in the association's efficiency. Training and development is one means to help the association realize the full potential of its staff. By monitoring staff performance in training programs, supervisors can assess individual strengths and weaknesses, and this information can be invaluable when making future staffing decisions.

With today's emphasis on personal growth, participation in a training and development program will give the employee an increased feeling of competence. The employees' acquisition of new skills and knowledge, resulting in increased productivity and improvements in the quality of their work, ultimately raises staff morale. Further, the offer of training and development can be incorporated into your association's benefit package and used as a tool for recruiting new employees.

Training and Development Methods

There are several commonly utilized methods of training and developing employees, each of which may be used in its entirety, in part, or in combination with one or more other methods, depending on the association's needs and organizational structure:

On-the-job-training is the most commonly used method for training and developing staff. It consists of the observation of a skill followed by the practice of the same skill. Some programs use manuals, formal demonstrations, problem-solving exercises, or charts in conjunction with an on-the-job training procedure. This type of training is usually geared to unskilled or semiskilled employees (clerical workers, machine operators) and is conducted by the employee's immediate supervisor or a more experienced staff member. The major advantage of on-the-job training is that the employee is trained under the actual working conditions of the job.

Simulation training takes place in an isolated area, usually a classroom or workshop, in which the actual working conditions of the job are duplicated. This method differs from on-the-job training in that it is removed from the work environment and thus places emphasis on learning, not production. Simulation training can be used to train several employees at the same time, and can be effectively supervised by someone who is a full-time staff trainer. Employees who generally benefit most from this type of training are typists, clerks, and machine operators.

Classroom training is especially useful for teaching theories, concepts, and problem-solving skills. Generally used to train technical, professional, and managerial staff, classroom training involves a formal, organized lecture format. Large numbers of staff can benefit at a relatively small cost; however, the trainees are passive observers, and practical application is not stressed. Since large numbers of employees are involved, the lectures must be geared to the lowest common denominator and higher level staff often do not receive the full benefit of training.

Conferences or formal meetings are organized around a specific theme or for a specific purpose. Many associations use conferences to set annual goals and objectives for their organization. Conferences are usually broken into small discussion groups with active participants. These groups are useful for information sharing and development of problem-solving skills, conceptual knowledge, and the formulation of attitudes. Participants should have some prior knowledge of the topic area in order to gain full benefit from the discussion. A major drawback of this method is that progress is often slow since all members who wish to speak are permitted to do so. This problem can be partially alleviated by the use of a group leader whose function is to channel discussion along the subject area.

The *case study* method of training and development is frequently used in law, personnel management, labor relations, and other human relations fields. Case studies describe an actual or hypothetical problem situation, and the trainees must identify the problems and propose solutions. This method is excellent for developing analytical skills and it encourages the integration of relevant material, some of which may have been learned previously in a classroom environment.

Other training and development methods include personal examples and role playing exercises. Learning by personal example is especially useful for acquiring managerial skills. A lower level employee will tend to imitate the behavior of a supervisor, especially when the employee sees the supervisor advance as a result of the behavior.

Role playing can develop and refine human relations skills by placing the trainees in roles as part of a hypothetical situation and having them interact accordingly. Employees learn-by-doing since they must decide on the appropriate behavior of a person in a particular position and under specified circumstances.

All the preceding methods can be used for either training or development programs. There are additional approaches for development programs for managerial staff.

An *understudy program* can provide an effective means to groom staff to fill upper-level management positions. The understudy serves as an administrative assistant to the manager and gradually acquires more responsibilities and duties from the manager until finally assuming the management position. Understudies often supervise small groups of employees. This method of development can be valuable to an association by helping it to develop a strong management resource. Also, the knowledge of who will occupy future positions can help to facilitate long-range planning and goal formulation. In addition, employees, with a promotion in sight, are usually motivated to perform well. The major disadvantage of the understudy approach is that it can perpetuate existing methods of management which may have become obsolete. As a result of learning precisely how to perform certain activities, the new employee's creativity can be stifled.

Job rotation or planned progression is sometimes used by associations with large staffs. Job rotation is designed to develop beginning-level managers by having them change jobs every three months to two years to familiarize them with all aspects of the association. This approach can be valuable to help the employees make decisions concerning their future goals and objectives by learning where their interests and talent lie. The association benefits from the opportunity to assess where each individual will be of optimum value to the organization. A disadvantage is the possibility of staff resentment toward the rotating executives.

Planned progression also involves job changes, but incorporates upward mobility in each change. Upper level managers often proceed through planned progression acquiring more duties and increased responsibility with each new position. This development method offers the developing manager an opportunity to get a broad perspective of the organization, and the first-hand knowledge gained through the progression may foster good relations with and an understanding of the lower level operations of the association. Upon attainment of the upper level position, the manager should be able to draw upon these experiences to make sound, efficient decisions, which take into account the functions and personalities of all those affected by the decision.

Other common staff development methods include committee assignments and sensitivity training. Regardless of the method or methods used for staff development, training should not be a one-time activity, but a continuous process tailored to meet the changing needs and goals of the association. By incorporating several of the described methods the association will have the flexibility to train and develop many staff members for all types of positions.

Performance Appraisal

Performance appraisal is potentially one of the most important management tools a professional association manager has at his or her disposal. Yet, traditionally, it is underutilized or misused. Instead of being used to help create pride in the association and a sense of personal satisfaction, performance appraisal has frequently created bitterness and suspicion among employees. This situation does not have to exist. There are many methods of performance appraisal that can achieve positive results for the association and its staff. Each association must select an approach that will meet the organization's particular needs.

Philosophy of Effective Performance Appraisal

In making a selection, it is important to recognize that a performance appraisal technique that creates fear of job security or fear of salary loss will not be a meaningful management tool. Few people are truly productive under conditions of continuous anxiety and stress. A performance appraisal process that provides an incentive for self-motivation and encourages commitment to the goals and objectives of the association will create an environment in which the staff can be productive.

The enlightened professional association manager will recognize that, given limited financial resources, a progressive and useful performance appraisal system will be one that offers more than economic gain or loss for the employees. The system should embody principles and concepts that foster individual growth and personal achievement. Few trade and professional associations will be able to motivate their employees with financial incentives alone. Not only is it probable that they will not have the financial resources to do so, but they will likely find that many employees will place an equal or higher premium on factors other than financial gains.

Methods of Performance Appraisal

In designing a performance appraisal system, the association should first establish objectives for the system. What should the performance evaluation indicate about the individual being appraised? What information is required to achieve the objectives of the appraisal process? The system objectives and the answers to these questions set the framework for the system design.

Several factors should be considered before proceeding with the specifics of an evaluation design. First, peformance appraisals should assess performance, not personalities. Evaluations which consider personal characteristics are often viewed as punitive by the employees being assessed. Second, the evaluation criteria must be tailored to the positions that will be appraised. Appraisal criteria for a typist are not appropriate for a manager since each position has unique characteristics and performance requirements.

Third, a good appraisal system will consider the representative aspects of the individual's performance, not exceptionally positive or negative behavior. In order to measure performance, the designer of the instrument must use a standard for comparison. This norm should be as objective as possible. It is helpful to consult with employees to be appraised during the development of the instrument. They can be helpful in determining standards and describing their responsibilities and duties. Their involvement in the design process will also help to remove the feelings of suspicion which usually arise at the time appraisals are conducted.

Performance appraisals may be conducted by one or more staff members. Multiple or group evaluations can be done by a panel of supervisors who are acquainted with the subject's work from different perspectives. This method is used for upper-level managers and emphasizes development needs. The panel evaluations are forwarded for review by the next line of authority who relates the appraisal to overall organizational effectiveness. The subject then confers with his or her immediate supervisor on the results. Suggestions are made for areas of needed improvement and development.

A third approach is self-appraisal. Self-appraisals are usually discussed with the immediate supervisor after completion. Surprisingly, studies have shown that employees are usually harsher on themselves in evaluations than an outsider would be. Some associations may combine group and self-evaluations with appraisals done by peers and supervisors. Peer/supervisor evaluations give a balanced profile of the individual and allow wide participation in the process.

Once the association determines who will evaluate the employee, it may select from a variety for performance appraisal methods. A number of the traditional methods are described below. Each method may be used alone or combined with others to ensure effective appraisal.

A review of production records is a very elementary method of measuring productivity. Limited in scope, objective production records measure quantity only, without considering behavior or quality of performance. Production records are suitable only for positions where easily identifiable units of work are produced.

Person to person comparisons involve a rank ordering of staff from the best employee to the worst employee. Each staff member's overall performance is compared with that of all others. These comparisons do not consider specific aspects of behavior and do not measure the amount of difference in performance from one employee to the next. The ranking process is highly subjective. Also, if a substantial number of people are involved in the comparison, the process may become extremely complicated.

Rating scales are the most commonly used method of assessing performance. Appraisal forms are used for the rating process. The ratings involve the listing traits and functions that are instrumental in determining the success or failure in a job and the identification of the degrees that denote strong or weak evidence of those factors in the employee's performance. *Exhibit VI-B*, at the end of the chapter, shows performance appraisal forms that use a rating scale. This type of appraisal process is straightforward, simple for staff to understand, and generally easy for supervisors to use. However, like most appraisal methods, it is highly subjective.

A *management by objectives process* is more complicated than a rating scale, and it requires considerably more preparation since the process serves as a planning and management technique as well as a performance appraisal mechanism. A management by objectives (MBO) system emphasizes the results achieved by the employee's performance, and it brings a high degree of objectivity to the appraisal. In an MBO system the employee and supervisor define individual goals and objectives for the employee in accordance with the goals and objectives of the association. Then they must meet regularly to discuss progress toward achievement of the objectives and to redefine the objectives if necessary. At the end of the year, performance is appraised on the basis of the degree to which the objectives have been achieved.

Many associations that have a management by objectives system also use a rating scale to assess a number of the critical traits and performance behaviors that are important in service organizations. In some cases this additional evaluation is necessary since staff members may achieve the objectives, but exhibit behavior that is not appropriate in the service environment of associations or that does not contribute to overall staff teamwork. To avoid the need for a supplemental rating process, many associations have employees establish personal development objectives that are designed to promote positive interpersonal behavior.

Narrative reports are used by many associations in evaluating staff performance. The performance reports may be structured by an outline or may be open-ended. They are written by someone who has full awareness of an individual's performance and attitudes, such as an immediate supervisor. All aspects of behavior that are considered by structured rating scales can be covered in written reports. However, narrative reports require considerable time and effort. And, unfortunately, the employee's appraisal may depend more on the evaluator's writing skills than on the employee's performance.

Critical incidence reports may be used to provide a profile of an employee's behavior, and to measure performance. A supervisor must first determine performance requirements for the staff member being appraised. Then the supervisor records any critical incidents that illustrate either excellent or poor performance by the employee. This method, as an ongoing process, consumes considerable time and effort, and it is narrow in focus since it reports only exceptional behavior, not average performance. In addition, if this method of appraisal is used, employees may believe that they are being observed constantly and may feel unduly pressured. This environment can be detrimental to good staff morale.

The performance appraisal process should be linked to the salary administration system as described in Chapter V. The results of the staff appraisals provide the basis for determining merit increases in staff salaries. Through this linkage the performance appraisal system becomes a valuable management tool.

Exhibit VI-A

APPLICATION FOR EMPLOYMENT

(Please use pen, PRINT all entries)

An Equal Opportunity Employer

IDENTIFICATION   Date _____ 19 ____

Name _____
          Last   First   Middle

Present
Address _____ How Long _____
          No. and Street   Apt.

                                              Home
_____ Phone No. _____
   City   State   ZIP

Have you ever worked for us before? Yes _____ No _____

Under what name? _____ When _____

Where _____

Position _____   When can you _____   Amount of _____
Wanted   start work   pay expected

PERSONAL INFORMATION

Are you over 18 years old? _____ If no, how old are you? _____

Are you a citizen of the United States or lawfully immigrated alien, legally eligible to work? _____

EMPLOYMENT EXPERIENCE / WORK HISTORY

Start with your present or your last employer. If you need more space, use an extra sheet of paper. If summer or part-time work, please indicate. If you were employed under a maiden or other name, please indicate that name by the employer.

May we request a reference from your present employer? _____ Yes. _____ No.

Name of employer _____ Phone No. _____

Address	City	State	ZIP Code
Type of Business	Starting date	Date of leaving	Your title and duties
Supervisor / Title	Starting pay	Pay at leaving	Reason for leaving

EXHIBIT VI-A (continued)

Name of employer _____ Phone No. _____

Address	City	State	ZIP Code
Type of Business	Starting date	Date of leaving	Your title and duties
Supervisor/Title	Starting pay	Pay at leaving	Reason for leaving

Name of employer _____ Phone No. _____

Address	City	State	ZIP Code
Type of Business	Starting date	Date of leaving	Your title and duties
Supervisor/Title	Starting pay	Pay at leaving	Reason for leaving

Is this a complete list of your employment? _____ Yes. _____ No.

STATEMENT

I understand that any misrepresentation in this application may constitute grounds for dismissal.

EDUCATION

List the schools you have attended.

	Name	Address	No. of Years	Year of Leaving	Graduate?	Grade Average	Course or Majors
Elementary							
High School							
Other							
College							
Post Graduate							

EXHIBIT VI-A (continued)

U.S. MILITARY SERVICE

List all service with dates and rank attained _____

_____

_____

_____

Describe any service duties or education which you feel relates to the position you want.
_____

REFERENCES

Please list three persons other than relatives and former employers who have known you for at least three years who can speak about your general character.

1. Name _____ Phone No. _____
   Street Address _____
   City, State, ZIP Code _____

2. Name _____ Phone No. _____
   Street Address _____
   City, State, ZIP Code _____

3. Name _____ Phone No. _____
   Street Address _____
   City, State, ZIP Code _____

PHYSICAL INFORMATION

Do you have any handicap which could substantially affect your performance in the position for which you are applying or which we should take into account in deciding for what position you are suited? _____ Yes. _____ No.

If "Yes," please explain _____

Are you willing to undergo a physical examination by our doctor at our expense? _____

EXHIBIT VI-B

STAFF PERFORMANCE APPRAISAL FORM
(Supervisory Exempt Staff)

Employee's Name: _____

Position Title: _____

Supervisor: _____

Period of Appraisal—From: _____ To: _____

Purpose of Appraisal:

☐ Probation

☐ Increment

☐ Promotion

☐ Termination or Resignation

	Outstanding	Superior	Satisfactory	Sub-Standard
A. Job Knowledge 1. Knowledge of present job				
2. Job-related background knowledge				
3. Knowledge of Society policies and procedures				
B. Supervisory capability				
C. Quality of Work				
D. Quantity of Work				
E. Initiative				
F. Dependability				
G. Cooperativeness				
H. Decision-Making and Execution				
I. Ability to work with Society members				
J. Identification with the Society's goals and objectives				
K. Effectiveness in Use of Resources				
L. Ability to Plan and Organize Work				

M. Capability of expressing ideas
  1. Orally
  2. In writing				

OVERALL APPRAISAL (Remarks on performance, strong points, weak points, training or additional education needed/recommended, recommended future assignments, changes in job content compared with job description, eligibility for promotion.)

Supervisor's Signature: _____ DATE: _____

Employee's Signature: _____ DATE: _____

* For Appraisal of Department-level or equivalent-level supervisors.

Exhibit VI-B (continued)

STAFF PERFORMANCE APPRAISAL FORM

(Non-Exempt Staff)

Employee's Name: _____

Position Title: _____

Supervisor: _____

Period of Appraisal—From: _____ To: _____

Purpose of Appraisal:

☐ Probation

☐ Increment

☐ Promotion

☐ Termination or Resignation

	Outstanding	Superior	Satisfactory	Sub-Standard
A. Job Knowledge				
1. Knowledge of present job				
2. Quality of job-related skills (typing, clerical, etc.)				
3. Capacity for added job-related responsiblities				
B. Quality of Work				
C. Quantity of Work				
D. Initiative				
E. Dependability				
F. Cooperativeness				
G. Organizational skills				
H. Ability to work with Society members (if applicable)				
I. Capability of expressing ideas orally or in writing (if applicable)				

OVERALL APPRAISAL (Remarks on performance, strong points, weak points, training or additional education needed/recommended, recommended future assignments, changes in job content compared with job description, eligibility for promotion.)

RECOMMENDED PERSONNEL ACTION

Supervisor's Signature: _____ DATE: _____

Employee's Signature: _____ DATE: _____

BIBLIOGRAPHY

The following books and cassette tapes are available from the American Society of Association Executives, 1575 Eye Street, N.W., Washington, D.C. 20005-1168, or by contacting Johnny Young, (202) 626-2748. Billing privileges are extended only to ASAE members and all orders for less than $15.00 must be prepaid.

Books

Association Executive Compensation Study. Washington, D.C.: American Society of Association Executives, 1987.
Cobb, William N. *How to Prepare a Personnel Policy Manual*. Holland, Mich.: C.R. & Associates, 1987.
Employment Contracts. Washington, D.C.: American Society of Association Executives, 1982. (Background Kit)
How to Write a Personnel Policy Manual. Washington, D.C.: Foundation of the American Society of Association Executives, 1987.
Job Descriptions for the Chief Executive Officer. Washington, D.C.: American Society of Association Executives, 1980. (Background Kit)
Performance Evaluation. Washington, D.C.: American Society of Association Executives, 1982. (Background Kit)
Personnel Policy Manuals. Washington, D.C.: American Society of Association Executives, 1983. (Background Kit)
Policies and Procedures in Association Management. Washington, D.C.: American Society of Association Executives, 1987.
Principles of Association Management. 2nd ed. Washington, D.C.: American Society of Association Executives, 1988.
Sample Job Descriptions. Washington, D.C.: American Society of Association Executives, 1982. (Background Kit)
Webster, George D. *The Law of Associations*. New York: Matthew Bender Co., 1975.

Cassettes

"The Art and Science of Surviving in a Small Association: The Generalist/Specialist," Charles D. Rumbarger, CAE; Marilyn Monroe, CAE: William Kelly, CAE, 1987.
"Building Top Performance by Setting Up an Effective Performance Appraisal System," Robert A. MacDicken and Ronald C. Pilenzo, 1987.
"A Complete Staff Orientation Package," Jeffrey J. Petro, 1987.
"Creating an Incentive Compensation Plan," Pat Alcorn, 1986.
"Employee Departures: Just One More Thing Before You Go. . ." Kenneth Bessette, 1987.
"Employment Law: What You Need To Know," Robert Alan Palmer, 1987.

"Evaluating the Evaluators: A Two-Way Communication Process," Ernest Stromberger, CAE, 1987.

"Hiring and Retraining Employees in the 21st Century," Steven J. Cabot, 1987.

"How to Give Performance Evaluations to Get Valuable Performance," Gary Richards, Sr., 1987.

"Interviewing Techniques for Applicant Truthfulness," Stanley M. Slowik, 1987.

"Maximizing the Partnership Between Staff and Volunteers," Jonathan Howe and Thomas A. Shannon, 1987.

"Policies and Procedures for Managing a Small Association," Barbara Byrd-Lawler, 1987.

"A Process for Planning Your Staffing Needs," Joyce A. Kozuch, Ph.D., 1987.

"Team Building: A Powerful Technique to Increase Productivity," David Jamieson, Ph.D., 1987.